The Peaceable Kingdom

A Primer in Christian Ethics

Second Edition

STANLEY HAUERWAS

scm press

© 1983 by University of Notre Dame Press,
Notre Dame, Indiana 46556
Postscript © 2003 by Stanley Hauerwas

British Library Cataloguing in Publication data
A catalogue record for this book is available
from the British Library

0 334 02933 3

First British edition published 1984 by SCM Press
9–17 St Albans Place, London N1 0NX
This new edition published 2003

www.scm-canterburypress.co.uk

SCM Press is a division of
SCM-Canterbury Press Ltd

Printed and bound in Great Britain by
Biddles Ltd, www.biddles.co.uk

The
Peaceable Kingdom

To the people
of the Broadway Methodist Church
for striving to be faithful
to the kingdom

Contents

Foreword

Who will help me decide what to do? And if ethicists are too busy building coherent systems to do so, at least Christian ethicists will respect our need for "concrete guidance in making and justifying a desicion."[1] Yet Stanley Hauerwas eschews such a responsibility from the outset. Or does he? Is it rather that the one who puts me through rigorous paces, helping me to *think out* my life as a Christian in our fragmented and violent world — that such a one is training me, as well as anyone can, to take the small steps which will cumulate in large decisions? And if that's not the way it works, it won't work at all, for decisions are not so much the sorts of things we do (or make) as they are more nearly made for us, yet in the end make us by shaping our subsequent lives.

So Hauerwas has long challenged our propensity to link ethics with "difficult decisions." Instead, he reminds us, what we can do is to help create a context more conducive to our deciding one way than another. Church promises to be that context: the social institution seeking to embody a specific configuration of virtues in its members. Christian ethicists can say what that configuration ought to look like and why. So their arguments will direct us to the sort of lives to which we would aspire, and the work that ought characteristically be ours. In this roundabout yet organic way, then, these ethicists will most certainly have helped us decide what to do — with our lives. Such is the art of Hauerwas's extended argument.

And it is, I shall argue, a thoroughly Catholic argument, in that sense which transcends "Roman" and increasingly includes Protestants who would participate in a long-standing tradition. For it locates the self firmly within a community, shaped in its freedom by the language and practices of that community, learning how to follow Jesus by continued schooling in that community's response. Moreover, it traces that response as the bishops first of South and now of North America have indicated: to Jerusalem, where Jesus confronts the powers of this world. It is a world comprised of those, including ourselves, who have chosen *not* to make this story of God their story. So the primary task of those who would make Jesus' story theirs is to stand within that world — their world — witnessing to a peaceable Kingdom which reflects the right understanding of that very world.

Such a stance will make stringent demands on those who would so follow Jesus. Much as Gandhi saw that a policy of *satyagraha* would require communities whose way of life would comprise training in nonviolent resistance, so Hauerwas argues for a church which could form its members in the virtues of patience and hope, as well as the capacity rightly to discriminate in particular situations. Again, it is not rules so much as practices which will guide us here: practices embodied in a community and justified through the continuing efforts of such a group to live up to its convictions. A new form of casuistry, if you will, and one which fleshes out the mini-narratives which characterized that phase of Catholic moral teaching, to make the process that much more formative in the lives of those who would follow Jesus — to Jerusalem.

Patience, with hope, will indeed be the virtues needed to grow up into the reality of a community witnessing to the peaceable kingdom. And here Hauerwas carries our appreciation of the virtues some steps further than his earlier writings. He makes explicit here how these are developed in relation with other persons. The peace that we can know, with ourselves, is the fruit of forgiving others, and forgiving others requires a context of truthfulness which assists us in shedding our illusions. Since that description could hardly characterize the world in which we live, it must depict the community we would form in the likeness of the kingdom Jesus preached and embodied.

In pursuing that task, moreover, we come to experience the joy associated with doing the *one thing* that is true! This fact adumbrates yet another dimension to the virtues of patience and hope: how they prepare us to live by the truth. Aquinas knew it as the contemplative life, and his teaching on the virtues required for living an active Christian life culminates in their predisposing us to contemplation.[2] The final pages of this exercise in understanding the Christian life do the same. For patience and hope assume the place they do in the program Hauerwas outlines for us, not simply because they help us to cope with the tragic gap between the world in which we stand and the kingdom to which we would witness. That they do, but they do so only because they are also at work to attune us to the reality of that world and that kingdom. If they empower us to confront evil, within and without, by nonviolent resistance, that is because they are also teaching us how to contemplate that truth which promises to make us free.

David B. Burrell C.S.C.

NOTES

1. John D. Barbour, "The Virtues in a Pluralist Context," *Journal of Religion* 63 (1983), 178.

2. *Summa Theologiae* 2.–2. 182; cf. my commentary in *Aquinas: God and Action* (Notre Dame, Ind.: University of Notre Dame Press, 1979), 165-167.

Preface

This book began at Hendrix College in Conway, Arkansas — the Athens of the South, as I was informed — where I had delivered a lecture and participated in a seminar on my work. In the process of spelling out a critique of contemporary philosophical and theological ethics, an undergraduate asked one of those simple questions that startle one into self-recognition, namely, what difference did my position make for how I taught my courses in Christian ethics? Much to my embarrassment, I had to admit that it did not make much difference, as I spent most of the time in my courses teaching other people's views. No doubt that has much to do with the ethos drummed into me from graduate school that my first responsibility was to present all sides of a question in the interest of scholarly fairness and objectivity. Yet that valid concern and task can too easily become a formula for intellectual cowardice and self-deception if it results in the assumption that as teachers we are released from the necessity of exposing our views to the critical response of students. So I returned home resolved to plan and teach a course shaped by my constructive proposals about how Christian ethics should be understood.

This book is the result of that resolve. I must begin, therefore, by thanking those undergraduates in my classes at Notre Dame who allowed me to test these ideas on them. I am also indebted to several summer school classes and institutes, such as those at Union Theological in Richmond, Virginia, and Iliff School of Theology, for providing me an opportunity to develop these reflections with more advanced students. From those students I have not only learned much about how to present my ideas, but their questions have often forced me to better understand what I want or need to say. As a result, I hope this primer bears the mark of actually having been taught and so will be more accessible for classroom use.

"Primers" or "introductions," of course, are notoriously hard to write. They are usually written either by younger scholars who think they know much more than is needed for such a trivial task, or by scholars toward the end of their careers who know they will never know enough but have gained the clarity to write with the simplicity and confidence that comes from knowing what they do not know. That I have attempted this "introduction" in mid-career probably indicates how little I have yet understood about Christian ethics. I have presumed to make the attempt simply because I am convinced Christian ethics is never the kind of reflection in which you ever "get it all straight," yet it is important that we try as best we can to introduce it to others. Thus, even though much in this book is underdeveloped, I hope at least some of those reading it will find the issues compelling enough to develop them more fully and/or show their inadequacy.

The title of the book is taken only indirectly from Scripture, as I was drawn to the text in Isaiah through Edward Hicks's paintings *The Peaceable Kingdom*. That many find these "primitive" presentations of Hicks compelling is due, I think, to the eloquence of simplicity. I only wish the pages of this book capture some of that eloquence and as a result the vision of God's peace might be formed more fully in us all. The less well-known work, *Noah's Ark*, also by Hicks, is perhaps even more powerful than his several portrayals of *The Peaceable Kingdom*. Hicks rightly saw the ark as an eschatological sign of peace, since only if the wolf was still able to lie down with the lamb would a saving remnant be possible. In this time when we are threatened by a flood of fire, I suspect we badly need Hicks's inspired vision. I hope this book may in some small way help engender and sustain such a vision.

As usual, I owe many for reading and criticizing earlier texts of this book. I owe a particularly heavy debt to my students: Mark Sherwindt, Phil Foubert, Paul Wadell, and Charles Pinches, who have not only criticized the content, but also the writing. Only they know how much they have taught me and in which areas I have not been able to respond sufficiently to all their criticisms. I also am indebted to my colleagues — James Burtchaell, John Howard Yoder, Robert Wilken — for their thoughtful criticisms. I only wish my thinking and writing were equal to the high standards of their criticism. Rowan Greer, Enda McDonagh, James McClendon, Jim Childress, and David Schmidt have also read the book and saved me from several obvious mistakes. My continuing indebtedness to Alasdair MacIntyre and David Solomon is obvious in the pages that follow.

The willingness of David Burrell to write a foreword to this book is but a testimony to my continuing debt to him. He is not only a constant source of inspiration, but he never fails to exercise his priest-ly office by reminding me never to take theology overly seriously.

As usual, I am indebted to James Langford, Director of Notre Dame Press, for first suggesting I needed to write a book along these lines and whose enthusiasm and patience has often kept me going. Also, I owe Ann Rice thanks for her continuing attempt to make my writing intelligible. Many told me my writing in a *Community of Character* had improved; little did they know I now had Ann Rice as an editor.

I must thank my wife and son, Anne and Adam, for their con-tinued support and the patience required for my writing and think-ing. Anne continues to correct my style; moreover she never fails to be unimpressed with what I think are "brilliant" ideas. As a result she makes me engage in the painful process of rethinking and revising what I thought I had right. But I owe Anne and Adam even more for their willingness to be present. We are self-absorbed beings, and there is something about writing that seems to make us particularly unaware of our self-involvement. I owe my family much, but no gift is more important than their constant demand that I see them as God's own rather than just further extensions of myself.

Finally, in the past I have made note of my ambiguous ecclesial position. While I am intellectually in no clearer position, I have at least over the past few years been part of a group of people who have been willing to claim me as part of their life—namely, Broadway Methodist Church in South Bend, Indiana. I am particularly in-debted to John Smith, the pastor at Broadway, for challenging me to become part of a concrete community. Because the people at Broad-way never cease to strive to be peaceable, I dedicate this book to them.

Introduction

1. INTRODUCING AN "INTRODUCTION"

While this book is meant to be a primer or introduction to Christian ethics which I hope can be used both in introductory courses in college and by adult study groups, I am not providing a survey of what various ethicists think on current issues in the field. Nor will I offer any extensive analysis of past and current figures in Christian ethics. Instead this book is an introduction in the sense that it attempts to present one straightforward account of a Christian ethic.

Alternative accounts are mentioned only as a means of clarifying my own position. As a result the book may be said to be decidedly "one-sided" for an introduction. My only defense is that I know no other way it can be done. As I try to show throughout, there is no way to do Christian ethics neutrally, since there is no agreement on what Christian ethics is or how it should be done that does not involve substantial theological and philosophical disagreements. Therefore I have not tried to write a text in the mode of William Frankena's *Ethics*. Rather this "introduction" is closer to Bernard Williams's *Morality: An Introduction to Ethics*, since, like him, I make no attempt to offer an account of what makes ethics ethics.

No one can doubt the usefulness of Frankena's careful distinctions and descriptions of various alternatives in ethical reflection. Yet his book leaves the unfortunate impression that ethics mainly involves the choice of one or a mixture of alternative ethical theories against others. In contrast, Williams's book reminds the student (and teacher) that ethics is never finally a matter of theory; rather, it is a reflective activity not easily learned. In the same spirit I have not assumed that on finishing the book readers will feel they know what "ethics" is or agree with the position I develop, but I do hope that they will be convinced that the activity exhibited in the book is one worth continuing. Moreover I hope that by working through the book they will develop some skills that will assist in their continuance of that activity or at least they will know where the issues and problems lie for thinking about — and living — a Christian ethic.

Such a disclaimer does not mean, however, that I am indifferent to the position developed in this book. I care, and deeply so, that the reader might come to appreciate, if not agree with, the stress on the centrality of nonviolence as the hallmark of the Christian moral life. I hope to show such a stance is not just an option for a few, but incumbent on all Christians who seek to live faithfully in the kingdom made possible by the life, death, and resurrection of Jesus. Nonviolence is not one among other behavioral implications that can be drawn from the gospel but is integral to the shape of Christian convictions.

In this book I also introduce themes I have touched on in my past work — i.e., the significance of virtue and character, narrative as a mode of moral reflection, the centrality of the life of Jesus for shaping the Christian life. Therefore it is an introduction to *a* Christian ethic. Yet I do not intend to present just my "personal views," but want to argue that the position I develop should be any Christian's. For it is my hope that the mode of analysis I present does justice to the shape of Christian convictions as they are found in Scripture, tradition, and the continuing lives of those who seek to live in a manner faithful to God's kingdom.

Because most of my previous work is in essay form many have suggested I need to "pull it all together" in one book. In some ways such a suggestion, while perfectly legitimate, is a bad idea. Not only do I have no idea of how I can "pull it all together," but more importantly, I would still maintain that an attempt at a summary distorts my basic understanding of theology. Theology cannot be construed by one overarching doctrine or principle. As I try to show, theology's inherently practical character, its unmistakable status as a pastoral discipline, simply defies strong systematization.

Of course I believe that theology involves a systematic display and analysis of Christian convictions and their relation to one another. Moreover, I think the theologian must try to show through the analysis of such relations in what sense Christian convictions can claim to be true. While I do not claim to have "pulled it all together" in this book, I try to make more explicit than I have in the past the conceptual foundation underlying the suggestions I have made about how theology, and in particular Christian ethics, should be done.

For those acquainted with my past work, I suspect the most surprising development in this book will be the emphasis I place on non-

violence. Many have viewed my pacifism with a good deal of suspicion, seeing it as just one of my peculiarities. Such an interpretation
is not unjust, since I have not written in a manner that exposes its
centrality. I hope this book will help make clear why it is so methodologically crucial as I try to show why a position of nonviolence entails,
for example, a different understanding of the significance of Jesus'
life, death, and resurrection than that offered in other forms of Christian ethics. Indeed, nonviolence is not just one implication among
others that can be drawn from our Christian beliefs; it is at the very
heart of our understanding of God.

To make nonviolence a central issue in an introductory book
may seem the worst possible strategy. It gives the impression that
the Christian moral life involves only this one thing, and surely that
is not the case. However, I hope to show how peaceableness as the
hallmark of Christian life helps illumine other issues, such as the
nature of moral argument, the meaning and status of freedom, as
well as how religious convictions can be claimed to be true or false.
As a result I do not concentrate on the theme of peace in the first part
of the book and even in the later parts peace is discussed only in relation to other theological issues. I hope this will make it clear that for
Christians peace is not an ideal known apart from our theological
convictions; rather the peace for which we hunger and thirst is determined and made possible only through the life, death, and resurrection of Jesus Christ.

The reader will find this work to be as much about theology as
about ethics. One of its major concerns is to show why Christian
ethics is a mode of theology. Indeed, to begin by asking what is the
relation between theology and ethics is to have already made a
mistake. Christian convictions are by nature meant to form and illumine lives. Since I hold that ethics is theology, in this book I
sometimes treat issues, such as the authority of Scripture or the relation of reason and revelation, that are generally reserved for systematic or philosophical theology. I cannot pretend to provide an adequate account or analysis here of these, and other, complex issues,
but I hope I say enough to show that such issues cannot be avoided
if Christian ethics is at the heart of the theological enterprise.

The first few chapters are an attempt to develop the conceptual
tools necessary to sustain this contention. Thus I emphasize narrative,
character, the virtues, and tradition as crucial for the explication of
the Christian life. These are familiar themes in my previous work, but
it is my hope that fresh light will be thrown on them here by my explicit attempt to investigate their interconnection.

I also try to take the many good criticisms of my past work into account. I hope that what I write indicates that I have learned much from such criticism, even though many of my critics may feel I respond unsatisfactorily to their concerns. That I do so is often because I simply do not know how to respond. For example, I continue to struggle with the problem of displaying the nature of agency and its relation to character. However, I do not respond positively to some criticisms of my work because I believe they widely miss the mark. Nevertheless, I hope it is clear that I very much value criticism, as it helps me state more exactly what I think and awakens me to the significance of such disagreement.

I may attempt to do the impossible in this book in that I wish it to be of as much interest to those who have not done a great deal of work in theology as to those who have. For the former, I hope that by following how one person construes the relation between various Christian convictions they will get some idea of what theological reflection involves and why it can properly claim integrity as an intellectual enterprise. Moreover, I hope they will gain the confidence thereby to try to work in theology better than I have been able to do and to see it as an exciting intellectual endeavor that is as enjoyable as it is important.

For the more seasoned, the book may help clarify my position, insofar as my "position" has clarity, and suggest in what ways I represent a somewhat unique theological alternative. Uniqueness or creativity are not in themselves virtues in theology, since the theologian's task is to serve a tradition and a community. Our freedom, and especially our intellectual freedom, comes from such service. Yet, when one serves a tradition that has at its center a crucified God, it is impossible to avoid the continuing challenge that is put to our imagination.

Though some may find my position at some points quite conservative and at others very liberal, I have no real interest in the labels and hope merely to say what I believe to be true to the character of the God who would have us live as a people of truth and peace in a violent world. I do not know if it is liberal or conservative to argue that theology cannot begin a consideration of ethics with claims about creation and redemption, but must begin with God's choice of Israel and the life of Jesus. Nor do I know if it is liberal or conservative to claim that the first social task of the church is to be the church, which entails being a community capable of being a critic to every human pretension. Theology is not a matter of being liberal or conservative but a matter of truth. I hope this book will illumine why and how this is so.

2. ON WHAT I OWE TO WHOM

The fact that my position is not easily characterized or located in relation to other theologians, past and present, has been a problem for some. Moreover, because I have not worked self-consciously as a Protestant or Catholic my work is all the more confusing. As a result some have suggested that I try to spell out my intellectual development. Again, I have doubt about such a project, since I am not at all sure whether I can provide an accurate account, and I fear such an attempt will call attention to the thinker rather than the thought. Nevertheless, I will try to draw some broad strokes in the hope they may provide the background for a better understanding of the position I develop in this book.

Those familiar with the intellectual currents in theology and philosophy over the last fifty years will rightly recognize that my position is far from original. I have learned and borrowed much from the Niebuhrs, Karl Barth, Paul Ramsey, James Gustafson, Fred Carney, John Howard Yoder, Alasdair MacIntyre, as well as many classical figures of the past such as Aristotle, Aquinas, Augustine, Calvin, Wesley, and Edwards. It may be less evident that I have learned much from John Dewey, R. G. Collingwood, and Ludwig Wittgenstein, as well as Plato. Though deeply dependent on all these thinkers, I hope I have avoided any crude eclecticism. I have never been interested in how thinker X relates to Y; rather my overriding concern has been systematic—namely, to understand how Christian convictions can claim to be true without distorting or giving a reductionistic account of what in fact Christians ought to believe.

In that respect one biographical point may be of some use. Though I was raised in a Christian home and grew up in the church, I never felt I knew well enough what Christianity involved to accept or reject it. I went through a time in college when I was sure Christianity could not be true. Then, through the study of philosophy, and under the gentle proddings of John Score, I came to realize I did not understand Christianity well enough to deserve an opinion. Indeed, I still often feel that is the case. I mention this only to point out that I have never felt the need to react against Christianity in the way many seem to do whose background provided more confidence that they knew in fact what Christianity involved both as belief and behavior. For me it has always been more a matter of trying to understand what we Christians should believe and do.

I went to seminary convinced that the discipline best suited for allowing one to pursue the question of the truthfulness of Christianity was systematic theology. In particular I wanted to concentrate on the "problem of history" (which turned out to be a tangle of "problems") as a way to understanding what it could possibly mean for God to act in history and, in particular, in the person of Jesus. Prior to the seminary I had become fascinated with R. G. Collingwood's analysis of historical investigation and construction, and correlatively of human action, and as a result was sure any account of Jesus' life and its relation to our own involved questions of historical explanation and human activity.

However, under the tutelage of Julian Hartt I became increasingly skeptical about the very idea of "systematic" theology. Indeed, the more I pondered not so much what Barth said about how to do theology, but how he did it, I became convinced that the idea of "system," at least in the nineteenth-century sense of system, distorted the ad-hoc character of theology as a discipline of the church. Moreover, confronted by the philosophical challenge concerning the "verifiability" of theological claims, I became convinced that while such a challenge often unhappily included positivist assumptions, it was nonetheless legitimate. Yet I was sure any adequate response would require attention to the practical force of theological convictions. So I decided to study Christian ethics. At least such an activity was committed to trying to provide a means to suggest what difference Christian convictions make in how we live — and thus how they might be false or true. My interest in Christian ethics, I suspect, also came from the then unacknowledged but powerful and continuing influence of the emphasis on sanctification in my Methodist heritage.

During this time I began to read much more extensively two quite different thinkers, H. Richard Niebuhr, who died the year before I went to seminary, and Ludwig Wittgenstein. The former, I found, had already long been at work on the agenda I thought I had discovered. Niebuhr was a theologian who did ethics only because it provided the means to explicate the intelligibility of theological convictions in terms of their practical force. Moreover I was convinced that Niebuhr was on the right track in his attempt to provide a phenomenology of moral experience truthful both to human existence and to the Christian understanding of our relation to God, even if I disagreed with some of his more "liberal" theological presuppositions.

The Niebuhr to whom I was attracted was the Niebuhr of *The Meaning of Revelation*. In that book Niebuhr wrestled hard with Christological issues. His distinction between inner and outer history seems to me to cause more trouble than it is worth. Nonetheless, he had his hand on the right problems. Given this, it puzzled me that the Niebuhr of *The Meaning of Revelation* could write *Radical Monotheism and Western Culture*, since the God of the latter seemed to lack the characteristics necessary to be identified with a particular people and their distinct history. Perhaps the tension between the positions of those two books witnessed to the tension in Niebuhr's life between the particular and universal, the historical and transcendent, the church as sect and as universal. While at present I wish to challenge the either/or implied by these polarities, I was convinced then that these were the alternatives. And if I were forced to choose between the two sides of Niebuhr's thought, I would take my stand on the side of particularity. Otherwise, I simply did not see how one could make sense of the significance of the life and death of Jesus for Christian life and thought. That is not to say that I wished to continue to do "Christology" in terms of classical categories. Under the tutelage of Hans Frei, and continuing to read Barth, I came increasingly to appreciate how the more "orthodox" Christologies failed to do justice to the scriptural portrayal of Jesus. Indeed my first interest in narrative was sparked by the realization that the early church thought that narrative was the appropriate mode of expression for what they took to be the significance of Jesus.

Wittgenstein's influence was of quite a different order than H. Richard Niebuhr's. He slowly cured me of the notion that philosophy was primarily a matter of positions, ideas, and/or theories. From Wittgenstein, and later David Burrell, I learned to understand and also to do philosophy in a therapeutic mode. But there were also substantive matters to be learned from Wittgenstein. Originally sparked by my interest in history, I had begun to work on issues in the philosophy of mind such as the relation of "mind-body problem," "intentionality," and "motivation." Wittgenstein (and Ryle and Austin) helped me see that "mind" did not relate to body as a cause to effect, for "mind" was not a singular thing or function. Moreover, Wittgenstein ended forever any attempt on my part to try to anchor theology in some general account of "human experience," for his writings taught me that the object of the theologians' work was best located in terms of the grammar of the language used by believers.

Because of these theological and philosophical interests I was struck by James Gustafson's suggestion that theological ethics might best focus on character and the virtues for displaying the nature of Christian moral existence. The issues underlying an account of character in moral psychology seemed to be precisely those that helped one to understand Jesus' life and its significance for us. It occurred to me that the correlation between our knowledge of God and of self, a correlation so well displayed by Calvin, might best be expressed in terms of character and the virtues.

Armed with this hunch I began a serious study of Aristotle and Aquinas. Contrary to the stereotypes, I found them remarkably congenial thinkers who assisted me in making many of the philosophical and theological moves I needed to develop my theological agenda. Interestingly, I did not find Aquinas to be first and foremost a "natural law ethicist," but one who saw how the theological virtues could help us understand and shape our lives.

Moreover I was increasingly convinced that unless Aristotle's and Aquinas's approach to ethics was recovered there was no way to break the impasse, and largely distracting debate, occasioned by Joseph Fletcher's, *Situation Ethics*. For that debate in no way suggested how our more positive theological convictions make sense only as they form our lives. Donald Evans's use of Austin's analysis of "performatives" to illumine claims of creation seemed to me to be the kind of constructive analysis we needed (even though Evans no longer thinks so), because such a perspective opened up the whole gamut of theological claims for ethical construal rather than concentrating on the "moral upshot" of our beliefs such as "love" or "justice." In my first work, *Character and the Christian Life*, I tried to show that by explicating the notion of character we could get a better idea of how Christian convictions are meant to inform our lives.

However the analysis of character I provided there was far too formal and abstract. Emphasis on character and the virtues countered the theological and ethical occasionalism so prevalent in theology and ethics, but the material content of character remained largely underdeveloped. While in *Character and the Christian Life* I used the theme of sanctification to spell out the nature of Christian character more concretely, I was still largely depending on secondary theological notions rather than displaying how more basic Christian convictions make, or should make, a difference.

In all honesty, I suspect I was too immature to know what my own religious convictions were or what those I had might entail. After all, surely my Ph.D. in ethics from Yale freed me from the need to have substantive convictions. I had something better — a professional vocation to help others see the implications and/or inconsistencies in their substantive convictions. Indeed it would be fascinating to study why so many of us who become "ethicists" work to transform that task from advocacy to parasitic theological analysis.

Two things soon suggested to me that being an "ethicist" involved more than being an expositor of the logical and behavioral implications of religious discourse. First, I began my teaching career at the height of the Vietnam War, and, second, I began to read the novels and philosophy of Iris Murdoch. Murdoch's powerful critique of contemporary philosophy's pretensions to objectivity in the name of analysis seemed to me decisive. Moreover, her emphasis on vision as the hallmark of the moral life struck me as exactly what was missing from most accounts of the virtues. While I had some difficulty with Murdoch's account of how we come to see, in particular her Platonic tendency to treat language as always distorting truthful vision, she nonetheless helped me understand how the virtues teach us to see the world without illusions or false hopes.

At the same time I was increasingly troubled by the challenge of the Vietnamese War. I had left graduate school assuming that some account of realism, such as Reinhold Niebuhr's, was the best one could find in Christian social ethics. While Niebuhr's understanding of justice was a bit intuitive for my taste, I thought it would be adequately supplemented by the development of more discriminating moral norms—such as Ramsey's account of just war—to help guide social policy. Yet I discovered the Niebuhrian position was inadequate to provide the resources to critically understand Vietnam.

Moreover I had continued to read in social and political theory. As a result I became increasingly aware of the insufficiency of Niebuhr's realism to the degree that it implicitly legitimated pluralism and balance of power as the norms of a good polity. Attacks on the "bias of pluralism" by such people as Robert Paul Wolff and Ted Lowi applied as much to Niebuhr as to the political scientist, but those critiques led me to see a more profound issue. The question I put to Niebuhr did not simply concern the status of certain theories of pluralist democracies, but the very status of liberalism as the primary public philosophy of America. For the first time I began to understand and appreciate the power of some of the Marxist critiques of America. As a result Reinhold Niebuhr appeared to me, despite his brilliant critique of American optimistic liberalism and romanticism, as a paradigmatic American liberal. The more I worried through this set of issues, the more I felt that any constructive Christian social ethic would have to find a way to recover a church with an integrity of its own rather than simply an institution designed to make "democracies" work better.

In the midst of all this I began to see that some of my uneasiness with Reinhold Niebuhr was the result of my emphasis on character and virtue. Drawing on the theme of justification, Niebuhr provided little place for the possibility of growth in the Christian life. What Niebuhr lacked, and what growth in character and virtue demanded, was a corresponding community of character and virtue. Gradually I saw that my attempt to develop an ethic of virtue might have sectarian implications I had not anticipated.

At that time I moved to the University of Notre Dame. There for the first time I encountered and began to take seriously the work of John Howard Yoder, who was then teaching at the Mennonite Seminary in Elkhart, Indiana and who now is at Notre Dame. The more I read of Yoder's scattered essays, the more I began to think he represented a fundamental challenge to the way I had been taught to think of "social ethics." Surprisingly, Yoder's account of the church fit almost exactly the kind of community I was beginning to think was required by an ethics of virtue.

However, Yoder was a pill I had no desire to swallow. His ecclesiology could not work apart from his understanding of Jesus and the centrality of nonviolence as the hallmark of the Christian life. The last thing I wanted to be was a pacifist, mainly because I longed to do ethics in a way that might be widely influential. Moreover by disposition I am not much inclined to nonviolence. But the more I read of Yoder the more I was convinced that the main lines of his account of Jesus and the correlative ethic of nonviolence were correct. I was also slowly coming to see that there was nothing very passive about Jesus' form of nonviolence, rather his discipleship not only allowed but required the Christian to be actively engaged in the creation of conditions for justice and peace.

But Yoder did something else for me. His emphasis on the significance of Jesus' whole life — that is, his teachings as well as his death and resurrection — provided me with the means to make my account of character and virtue less formal. I was able to return to my original project with fresh vision. I had perhaps discovered a way, for example, to appreciate without piously distorting Mark's powerful development of discipleship, which takes Jesus' life to be a paradigm for our own lives.

My struggle with Yoder's position also helped me to articulate my growing conviction that there was something deeply distorting about the ahistorical character of modern ethics. Philosophical advances in epistemology and the philosophy of science, as well as my developing theological convictions, convinced me that theology (and ethics) did not need an ahistorical "foundation." Bernard Williams

and Alasdair MacIntyre, in their critiques of contemporary philosophical ethics, helped me see, however, that to abandon the search
for a "foundation" does not necessarily entail the loss of rationality
in ethics (or anything else). Moreover MacIntyre continued to build a
constructive alternative that provided for a fruitful appreciation of
the positive significance of the church with regard to both methodological and social ethical questions.

One emphasis in my work remains yet unexplained—that is,
narrative—from whence did it come? I honestly do not know. Certainly I had been pondering the significance of narrative both in
terms of issues in theology that Frei and Hartt had raised and in terms
of the philosophy of mind and action. The more I thought through
the problem of describing intentional action, the more I was convinced that narrative was a crucial concept for displaying agency. And
of course the stress on character in terms of a perduring agency entailed a narrative dimension.

As I worked at finding a way to solidify all these themes, I found
that narrative proved to be an extraordinarily fruitful concept. Unfortunately it also constantly threatens to become a catch word for a new
theological fad. I hope it is clear, therefore, that it has never been,
nor is it now, my intention to develop a narrative theology or a
theology of narrative. I do not know what either would look like.
Theology itself does not tell stories; rather it is critical reflection on
a story; or perhaps better, it is a tradition embodied by a living community that reaches back into the past, is present, and looks to the
future. Hence, it is a mistake to assume that my emphasis on narrative is the central focus of my position—insofar as I can be said even
to have a position. Narrative is but a concept that helps clarify the
interrelation between the various themes I have sought to develop in
the attempt to give a constructive account of the Christian moral life.

That ends, at least to this point, my understanding of what I
owe to whom. I fear it is at once too simple and too complex. The
influence of such people as James McClendon, Robert Wilken,
Joseph Blenkinsopp, and David Burrell has not been adequately acknowledged. Nor have I explored how my more "practical" concerns,
such as the place of the retarded, have influenced my more basic
methodological concerns. However I hope this account helps some to
better understand the project I have been developing, even if they remain unconvinced by the position I take in this book. At the least
I hope to have made it clear that my "originality" is not properly so
called, since most of my ideas I borrowed from others.

3. MY ECCLESIAL STANCE

At the risk of testing my reader's patience beyond limit, there is one last issue that I feel I must say a word about—namely, do I write as a Catholic or as a Protestant? The answer is that I simply do not know. I do not believe that theology when rightly done is either Catholic or Protestant. The object of the theologian's inquiry is quite simply God—not Catholicism or Protestantism. The proper object of the qualifier "catholic" is the church, not theology or theologians. No theologian should desire anything less than that his or her theology reflect the catholic character of the church. Thus I hope my theology is catholic inasmuch as it is true to those Protestants and Roman Catholics who constitute the church catholic.

Of course the fact I am biographically a Protestant is not irrelevant to the way I work. I have no desire to rid myself of my particular background as an evangelical Methodist. Rather it is my conviction that Methodism, like other Christian traditions, with its limits and possibilities, helps awaken all of us to being members of Christ's whole church. Thus, even if I am critical of my tradition, I am rightly so only so long as that criticism serves to direct Protestants and Catholics alike to the one Lord who reigns over all people.

1. Christian Ethics in a Fragmented and Violent World

1. ETHICS AND THE DEMAND FOR ABSOLUTES

All ethical reflection occurs relative to a particular time and place. Not only do ethical problems change from one time to the next, but the very nature and structure of ethics is determined by the particularities of a community's history and convictions. From this perspective the notion of "ethics" is misleading, since it seems to suggest that "ethics" is an identifiable discipline that is constant across history. In fact, much of the burden of this book will be to suggest that ethics always requires an adjective or qualifier—such as, Jewish, Christian, Hindu, existentialist, pragmatic, utilitarian, humanist, medieval, modern—in order to denote the social and historical character of ethics as a discipline.[1] This is not to suggest that ethics does not address an identifiable set of relatively constant questions—the nature of the good or right, freedom and the nature of human behavior, the place and status of rules and virtues—but any response to these questions necessarily draws on the particular convictions of historic communities to whom such questions may have significantly different meanings.

That ethics is an activity relative to particular times, places, and communities may seem obvious, but it is also easily forgotten and its significance ignored. We each feel a powerful desire to claim that the ethic that guides us is free from historical relativity and/or arbitrariness. After all, morality often deals with matters that entail sacrifices by ourselves and others, and we think such sacrifices can only be justified on the basis of unchanging principles.

Thus it is often thought that one of the primary tasks of ethics is to show how morality is grounded in unchangeable principles and convictions. Many assume, moreover, that the best way to ensure the unchangeableness of our principles is to claim that they are sanctioned by God. We can be sure of our principles if they can be shown

1

to rely upon God's will. Because of this, some have claimed that if God does not exist everything is morally permissible. Though such a claim belies the complexity of the relation of religious convictions to morality, many believers and unbelievers alike seem to think that if God does not in some manner underwrite the absoluteness of our moral system we will not be able to say what is wrong with murder, or lying, or stealing, etc.

As a Christian ethicist I am often asked "Aren't there any absolutes anymore?" The questioners tend to assume that if the answer is "no," then ethics has simply ceased to exist. They assume this even though it is by no means clear to what their term "absolute" applies — to values, or rules, or convictions — or even if such absolutes have anything to do with Christian beliefs and practices.

To persons who hold this view, my claim that ethics always requires a qualifier seems an abdication of responsibility. They see the task of the ethicist in our time as that of reasserting the continued viability of those absolute norms that are not dependent upon a particular people's history, in order to sustain the moral character of our way of life. I maintain that such a view of ethics is radically misconceived, and particularly so for ethics done in a Christian context. But before suggesting why that is the case, we must try to understand the reasons behind the hunger for absolutes in our time.

2. LIVING AMID FRAGMENTS: THE INSUFFICIENCY OF ETHICS

One of the ironies of the current situation is that the attempt to *deny* that ethics responds to the peculiarity of our current social and historic situation only makes us more subject to that situation. We are told we live in a morally bankrupt age. People think what was at one time unthinkable; indeed they *do* what was once unthinkable. We experience our world as so morally chaotic that we now feel our only alternative is for each person "to choose," if not create, the standards by which they will live.

As pervasive as this feeling is, it is unclear exactly why we feel we are morally at sea. No time or society has ever been free of moral ambiguity. Why should we feel that some decisive change has occurred in our own time? Indeed, are we sure our values have changed, or is it their institutional settings? For example, we may still value the family, but may now have quite a different understanding of what we mean by "the family." Simply quoting divorce statistics does not suffice to show that we are morally confused about, or no longer value, the family. Such statistics may be an indication that people have found the traditional commitments of marriage merely over-zealous. Perhaps the moral force of marriage can be sustained in other settings; for example, maybe there is no inherent incompat-ibility between marriage and sex with more than one person.

I suspect that the experience of the world as morally adrift has a more profound source than the mere observation that people are permitted to do what was once unthinkable. Our disquiet about mor-ality more likely arises from within us. Even though we feel strongly about abortion, divorce, dishonesty, and so on, we are not sure why we feel as we do. And the less sure we are of the reasons for our beliefs, the more dogmatically we hold to them as our only still point in a morally chaotic world. Ironically, our dogmatism only masks our more profound doubt, for although we hold certain moral convic-tions adamantly, we secretly suspect that we believe what we do because we have been conditioned. We hold certain beliefs as if they are unconditioned, yet are impressed with the knowledge that all beliefs are the result of environment, and thus at least potentially ar-bitrary. That very acknowledgment seems then to reduce all moral disagreements to subjective opinions about which there can be no argument.

This lurking suspicion that we really have no firm grounds for our beliefs makes us all the more unwilling to expose what we think to critical scrutiny. We thus take refuge among others who think as we do, hoping sheer numbers will protect us from the knowledge of our uncertainty. Or sometimes we suppose that if we think deeply and critically about our moral convictions, we will be able to supply adequate justification for what we believe. In both cases we assume that "ethics" must be able to provide the means for preventing our world from falling into a deeper moral chaos.

Underlying such a view or morality is the presupposition that we are required by our modern predicament to make up our "own minds" about what is good and bad. Indeed, those who do so with determination are seen as morally exemplary because they act autono-mously rather than uncritically accept convention. But the very no-tion we are "choosing" or "making up" our morality contains the seeds of its own destruction, for moral authenticity seems to require that morality be not a matter of one's own shaping, but something that shapes one. We do not create moral values, principles, virtues; rather they constitute a life for us to appropriate. The very idea that we choose what is valuable undermines our confidence in its worth.

In many ways the current popularity that "ethics" enjoys is odd, for most people most of the time would prefer not to have to think about what is the right or wrong thing to do. They simply want to get on with the living of their lives: to fall in love, raise families, have satisfying professions, support decent and worthwhile institutions.

Certainly there is something correct in our feeling that we are required to think too much about "ethics" today.[2] However, it is not that we are required to think—every society regardless of its "ethics" develops some forms of critical reflection about how best to act. Rather it is *what* we are required to think about. Contemporary ethics concentrates on moral quandaries: Should we lie to protect a friend? Is withholding the complete truth a form of lying? Must we tell a dying person he or she is dying? And so on. It thus appears that "ethics" is primarily concerned with ambiguous situations and hard decisions.[3] Such a concentration on "quandaries" obscures the fact that they make sense only in the light of convictions that tell us who we are. Our most important moral convictions are like the air we breathe: we never notice them because our life depends on them. For example, our concern with lying derives from the conviction that we should be truthful. Behind our current feeling of chaos lies the fact that very "air we breathe" is being questioned. I suspect that it is not that we have no moral guides, but that we have too many. As Alasdair MacIntyre has suggested, our problem is that we live amid fragments of past moralities each, with good reasons, competing for our loyalty. In order to understand the implications of this he asks us to:

> Imagine that the natural sciences were to suffer the effects of a catastrophe. A series of environmental disasters are blamed by the general public on the scientists. Widespread riots occur, laboratories are burnt down, physicists are lynched, books and instruments are destroyed. Finally a Know-Nothing political movement takes power and successfully abolishes science teaching in schools and universities, imprisoning and executing the remaining scientists. Later still there is a reaction against this destructive movement and enlightened people seek to revive science, although they have largely forgotten what it was. But all that they possess are fragments: a knowledge of experiments detached from any knowledge of the theoretical context which gave them significance; parts of theories unrelated either to the other bits and pieces of theory which they possess or to experiment; instruments whose use has been forgotten; half-chapters from books, single pages from articles, not always fully legible

because torn and charred. None the less all these fragments are reembodied in a set of practices which go under the revived names of physics, chemistry and biology. Adults argue with each other about the respective merits of relativity theory, evolutionary theory and phlogiston theory, although they possess only a very partial knowledge of each. Children learn by heart the surviving portions of the periodic table and recite as incantations some of the theorems of Euclid. Nobody, or almost nobody, realises that what they are doing is not natural science in any proper sense at all. For everything that they do and say conforms to certain canons of consistency and coherence and those contexts which would be needed to make sense of what they are doing have been lost, perhaps irretrievably.

In such a culture men would use expressions such as 'neutrino', 'mass', 'specific gravity', 'atomic weight' in systematic and often interrelated ways which would resemble in lesser or greater degrees the ways in which such expressions had been used in earlier times before scientific knowledge had been so largely lost. But many of the beliefs presupposed by the use of these expressions would have been lost and there would appear to be an element of arbitrariness and even of choice in their application which would appear very surprising to us. What would appear to be rival and competing premises for which no further argument could be given would abound.[4]

MacIntyre contends that in respect to its moral language the actual world we inhabit is very similar to the gravely disordered state of natual science in his imaginary world. "What we possess . . . are the fragments of a conceptual scheme, parts which now lack those contexts from which their significance derived. We possesss indeed simulacra of morality, we continue to use many of the key expressions. But we have—very largely, if not entirely—lost our comprehension, both theoretical and practical, of morality."[5] MacIntyre points out that the limit of this analogy between our world and his imaginary one is that we have no record of a similar catastrophe that has left our moral world so fragmented. All we have are its effects.

If MacIntyre is correct we live in a precarious situation. Life in a world of moral fragments is always on the edge of violence, since there are no means to ensure that moral argument in itself can resolve our moral conflicts. No wonder we hunger for absolutes in such a world, for we rightly desire peace in ourselves and in our relations with one another. Granted the world has always been violent, but when our own civilization seems to lack the means to secure peace within itself we seem hopelessly lost.

Moreover the fragmentation of our world is not only "out there," but it is in our own souls. Amid fragments it is extremely hard to maintain our moral identity. We feel pulled in different directions by our various roles and convictions, unsure whether there is or can be any coherence to our lives. We become divided selves, more easily tempted to violence since, being unsure of ourselves, we are easily threatened by any challenge that might rob us of what little sense of self we have achieved.

Lacking any habits or institutions sufficient to sustain an ethos of honor, we become cynical. By suspecting all, by assuming that behind every cause lies self-interest and behind every act of charity a psychological payoff, we hope to protect ourselves from being misused or lost. Yet cynicism inevitably proves too corrosive. Its acid finally poisons the self, leaving no basis for self-respect because it renders all activities unworthy of our moral commitment.

In such a world the emphasis of Christian ethics on the significance of the qualifier "Christian" appears to many to capitulate to the chaos. We need instead, they say, to reformulate a universal morality that is able to bring order to our fragmentary world, securing peace between and in ourselves. Yet such universality will not come if Christians fail to take seriously their particularistic convictions. We Christians who, as I hope to show, are inextricably committed to a peaceable world, believe that peace is possible only as we learn to acknowledge and serve the Lord of this world, who has willed to be known through a very definite and concrete history. Therefore, Christian ethics holds to the importance of its qualifier, because the peace Christians embody, and which they offer to the world, is based on a kingdom that has become present in the life of Jesus of Nazareth.

But faithfulness to such particularities strikes most as far too unreliable, and they continue the quest for a universal ethic that can insure certainty, if not peacefulness. I wish to claim, however, that such a quest only makes us more susceptible to violence. I must now try to show why such is the case.

2.1   Freedom as Fate

Our sense that we live in a morally chaotic, fragmented world accounts for two of the dominant characteristics of recent ethical theory: (1) the stress on freedom, autonomy, and choice as the essence of the moral life; and (2) the attempt to secure a foundation for the moral life unfettered by the contingencies of our histories and communities. As we will see, these are closely related insofar as it is assumed that freedom depends on finding the means to disentangle ourselves from our own engagements.

Caught between the competing interests, we increasingly feel compelled to create or choose our morality. This is variously reflected by moral theories such as emotivism, existentialism, and situationalism, which maintain that moral knowledge is not so much discovered as "created" through personal choice. Therefore the necessary basis of authentic morality is seen as the freedom to choose and willingness to take responsibility for choices.

Such a strong assertion of freedom seems a bit odd when we remember that one of our other dominant assumptions is that we are largely determined by our environment and biology. Indeed, one of the hallmarks of modernity is that we feel ourselves at once both determined and free. Peter Berger suggests an explanation for this glaring incompatibility in his *Heretical Imperative*.[6]

According to Berger, premodern people lived for the most part in a given world. They had little choice about where to live, what vocation to enter, or whom to marry. As a result, they were not hounded by our modern ambivalence. While premodern people may have struggled with the meaning of life, they did not need to question, as we seem required to do, whether their life was sufficiently coherent to legitimately ask its meaning.

Modern people, Berger contends, find themselves confronted not only by many possible courses of action, but also by many possible ways of thinking about the world. As a result all life has become consumer oriented. We choose not only between toothpastes, but between the very "plausibility" structures that give our lives coherence and meaning. Our need to choose even those basic beliefs about why things are as they are and not otherwise, suggests an arbitrariness about them which undermines truthfulness. Finally, the only thing we feel we can be sure of in such a world is the absolute necessity of our own autonomy. In fact, our deepest conviction, our surest "plausibility structure," is that if our lives are to have meaning we must create it.

We have thus been condemned to freedom, or as Berger prefers, the "heretical imperative." "For premodern man, heresy is a possibility—usually a rather remote one; for modern man, heresy typically becomes a necessity. Or again modernity creates a new situation in which picking and choosing becomes an imperative.''[7] Thus our ethical theorizing has led to the notion that freedom is not only a necessity but a moral ideal. Freedom itself is at once the necessary and sufficient condition of being moral.

But is this situation so unique? Haven't almost all moral theories held in different ways that people could only be responsible for what they have the power to do? Has not freedom always been thought crucial to moral behavior? Yet for philosophers such as Aristotle, freedom was not an *end in itself*; we became free only as we acquired the moral capability to guide our lives. To lack such capability was to be subject to the undisciplined desires and choices of the immature. Thus freedom did not reside in making choices but in being the kind of person for whom certain options simply were not open. For example, the courageous could not know the fears of the coward though they were required to know the fears appropriate to being courageous. Only the virtuous person could be free, insofar as freedom was not so much a status as a skill.

In contrast to our sense of "freedom of choice" the virtuous person was not confronted by "situations" about which he or she was to make a decision, rather the person determined the situation by insisting on understanding it not as a "situation" but as an event in a purposive narrative. Character determines circumstance, even when the circumstance may be forced upon us, by our very ability to interpret our actions in a story that accounts for moral activity.

In contrast, the modern conception has made freedom the content of the moral life itself. It matters not *what* we desire, but *that* we desire. Our task is to become free, not through the acquisition of virtue, but by preventing ourselves from being determined, so that we can always keep our "options open." We have thus become the bureaucrats of our own history, seeking never to be held responsible for any decisions, even for those we ourselves have made.

This attempt to avoid our history, however, results in the lack of the self-sufficiency to claim our lives as our own. For as we look back on our lives, many of the decisions we thought we were making freely, seem now to have been more determined than we had realized. We say: "If I only knew then what I know now." Using this as a means to claim nonresponsibility for our past, we imagine that *next time* we will really act "freely." As a result we tend to think the moral life and ethical reflection are concerned with prospective decisions and the securing of the conditions necessary to insure that those "decisions" will be free. We ignore the fact that the more important moral stance is retrospective, because it is in remembering and accepting that we learn to claim our lives as our own — including those decisions that in retrospect were less than free. Ironically, my freedom turns out to depend on my ability to make my own that which I did not do with "free choice" but which I cannot do without. For what we are, our sense of ourselves, rests as much on what we have suffered as what we have done.

The modern assumption that freedom is the necessary and sufficient condition of morality is not easily changed, for it also determines how we govern our social relations. Our society seems generally to think that to be moral, to act in a responsible way, is to pursue our desires fairly — that is, in a manner that does not impinge on anyone else's freedom. We assume we can do as we want so long as we do not harm or limit anyone else's choices. A good society is one that provides the greatest amount of freedom for the greatest number of people. Although such an ethic appears to be highly committed to the common good, in fact its supporting theory is individualistic, since the good turns out to be the sum of our individual desires.

Even more troubling than this individualism is the price we pay in holding this view of ourselves and others; the price is nothing less than a systematic form of self-deception. Insofar as we are people who care about anything at all, we necessarily impinge on the "freedom" of others. But we act as if we do not, thus hiding from ourselves and others the truth that we are necessarily tied together in a manner that mutually limits our lives. We have taught ourselves to describe our moral convictions as our "personal desires," implying thereby that they need not significantly affect others. In fact, however, there is *no* morality that does not require others to suffer for our commitments. But there is nothing wrong with asking others to share and sacrifice for what we believe to be worthy. A more appropriate concern is whether what we commit ourselves to is worthy or not.

As a result of our self-deception our relations have become unrelentingly manipulative.[8] We see ourselves and others as but pawns engaged in elaborate games of power and self-interest. I do not mean to suggest that there has ever been a time or social order from which manipulation was absent. What is new about our present situation is that our best moral wisdom can conceive of no alternative. We seem able only to suggest ways to make the game more nearly fair. We are unable to provide an account of a morality worthy of requiring ourselves and others to suffer and thus releasing us from the prison of our own interests.

Our stress on freedom and its ethical expression renders us incapable of accounting for certain activities which seem central to the human project. Consider something as simple as the decision to have children. In an ethics of freedom how can we justify such a decision when it clearly involves an imposition of our will and desires on that new life. No amount of good care and/or love could be sufficient to redress the imbalance of freedom in this situation. We have forced this being into existence to satisfy our desires! In the ethos of freedom the relationship between parents and children cannot help but induce resentment and the resulting bargaining games. We resent the time our children require of us and they resent the burden of guilt they feel for what appears to be our begrudging care for them. We are thus caught in a web of manipulation from which we seem unable to escape.

2.2   Fragile Foundations

Equally pervasive as the stress on freedom in modern ethical theory has been the concern to find a foundation for ethics. Indeed the attempt to provide a foundation for ethics is interrelated with the attempt to establish freedom as a prerequisite characteristic of human agents. As MacIntyre suggests, modern philosophers, both analytic and existentialist, have taken the essence of moral agency to be the capacity of the self to evade identification with any particular contingent state of affairs.

> To be a moral agent is, on this view, precisely to be able to stand back from any and every situation in which one is involved, from any and every characteristic that one may possess, and to pass judgment on it from a purely universal and abstract point of view that is totally detached from all social particularity. Anyone and everyone can thus be a moral agent, since it is in the self and not in social roles or practices that moral agency has to be located.[9]

Thus it has become the task of ethical theory to find a foundation free of historical contingencies that can guarantee the availability of such freedom for the agent.

The grand example of this project is, of course, the work of Immanuel Kant, who sought to ground morality in the very necessity of freedom. It was Kant's great enterprise to free morality from the arbitrary and the contingent, in order to secure at least minimal agreement between people of differing beliefs and societies. Moreover Kant tried valiantly to free the realm of morality from the determinism he thought characteristic of the natural world. He sought to guarantee the "autonomy" of morality by grounding morality neither in religious or metaphysical beliefs, nor in any empirical account of humanity, but in rationality *qua* rationality.

Kant contended that the distinctive moral characteristic of the rational creature was the capacity to live by no other law than that of its own making. Thus for Kant the autonomy of reason and the autonomy of morality rested on the same basis. This law, which Kant thought to be inherent in rationality, he called the categorical imperative, which requires we do our duty for no other reason than it is our duty. His first formulation of the categorical imperative was "Act only according to that maxim by which you can at the same time will that it should become a universal law."[10] While this principle, and its relation to Kant's other formulations of the law, has been variously interpreted and restated, it is generally accepted as the basic statement for justifying moral judgments, whether it is called the "principle of generalization" or, more existentially, "the moral point of view." The force of the principle stays the same: It renders the contingent history of the agent irrelevant in moral judgment and evaluation; it demands that the justification for our decisions be given from the perspective of anyone.

It is not my interest here to evaluate Kant's project or his later interpreters, but to observe how the general project of finding a foundation for morality has gone hand in hand with an aversion to the particular and the contingent. Why has ethics the sudden need for a "foundation" and in particular a foundation that is characterized by universality and necessity, when it seems that such a demand distorts the very nature of moral judgment? As Aristotle reminds us, ethics by its nature deals with matters which can be other—that is, particular matters.[11] Confronted by the fragmented character of our world, philosophers have undoubtedly tried to secure a high ground that can provide for security, certainty, and peace. It is a worthy effort, but one doomed to fail, for such ground lacks the ability to train our desires and direct our attention; to make us into moral people.

Despite enthusiasm of many religious thinkers for this search for a foundation for morality, such a foundation ironically cannot but make religious convictions morally secondary.[12] Here we stumble on a problem at least as old as Plato's *Euthyphro*, namely how do religion and morality relate? Is something right because God commands it, or because it is right? If the latter, then why do we need God to command it? I cannot here give adequate attention to this issue but only note that the discussion of it typically turns on a far too limited understanding of morality. As I will discuss later, those traditions that have emphasized natural law as one response to the problem have tended to relegate "religious" aspects of the moral life to a "higher" morality or to the motivational component of morality. As a result, not only has the moral force of Christian convictions been lost, but the very nature of moral experience has been distorted.

More significantly, when the particularity of Christian convictions is made secondary to an alleged more fundamental "morality," we lose the means to be a peaceable people. For the attempt to secure peace through founding morality on rationality itself, or some other "inherent" human characteristic, ironically underwrites coercion. If others refuse to accept my account of "rationality," it seems within my bounds to force them to be true to their "true" selves.

As Christians, we must maintain day in and day out that peace is not someting to be achieved *by our power*. Rather peace is a gift of God that comes only by our being a community formed around a crucified savior — a savior who teaches us how to be peaceful in a world in rebellion against its true Lord. God's peaceful kingdom, we learn, comes not by positing a common human morality, but by our faithfulness as a peaceful community that fears not our differences.

3. THE PRIVITIZATION OF RELIGION

Many of the same processes that have shaped our modern understanding of morality have had an equally strong and corrosive effect on our religious convictions and institutions. If religion is no longer considered a matter of truth, it cannot and should not command our attention as something worthy in and of itself. Rather religion's significance is reduced, at best, to the functional. Thus religious belief may be a source of strength in a personal crisis and/or an aid in interpersonal relations. Accordingly, the church has become but one among many voluntary associations of like-minded people from similar economic strata.

The functional character of contemporary religious convictions is perhaps nowhere better revealed than in the upsurge of religious conservatism. While appearing to be a resurgence of "traditional" religious conviction, some of these movements in fact give evidence of the loss of religious substance in our culture and in ourselves. Christianity is defended not so much because it is true, but because it reinforces the "American way of life." Such movements are thus unable to contemplate that there might be irresolvable tensions between being Christian and being "a good American."

At a more sophisticated level, many still seek to use our religious heritage in support of the development and sustenance of democratic government and society. Thus it is said that democracy requires a civil religion—that is, a sense of transcendence that can act as a critical principle against the pretensions of state power as well as a resource to support the development of more nearly just institutions. Such a "civil religion," however, cannot be made up of any particularistic religious beliefs, since that would offend the necessity of religious tolerance. As a result all our more particularistic beliefs must be socially defined as "private" and thus admitting of no social role. This situation creates a special irony, since the culture and political order that the "civil religion" is asked to underwrite requires a disavowal of the public role of religious conviction—thus supporting the assumption that our religious opinions are just that, opinions.[13]

There is no more powerful indication of religion's superfluity in our culture than Christianity's acceptance of itself as one "religion" among others. It reveals an assumption of the priority of so-called "faith" over particular convictions of the Christian faith, e. g., the nature of God, the significance of Jesus, the eschatological fate of the world.[14] As a result, Christianity, both in practice and in its sophisticated theological expression, is reduced to an interpretation of humanity's need for meaning or some other provocative anthropological claim. I do not mean to deny that every theology involves anthropological claims, yet theology today has become particularly adept at beginning and ending there. More than before we substantiate Feuerbach's claim that religion is but the projection of mankind's hopes written large.

Those concerned with the ethical significance of Christian convictions are particularly prone to this kind of anthropologizing of Christian theology. Acting on a suspicion that what is left of Christianity is its ethical component, they abstract the ethical from the religious in an effort to make Christianity relevant. Though such a strategy often appears theologically and ethically radical, it usually results in a restatement of the prevailing humanism in the name of religion.

Behind this form of modern religious apologetics lies the assumption that religion can have no hold on us unless it functions to underwrite our desires and ensure our ultimate happiness. There is, of course, a proper sense in which this is true, since the conviction that the kingdom wrought in Christ is meant to fulfill our deepest and strongest desires is at the heart of Christianity. Insofar as we are God's creatures his redemption is certainly the fulfillment of the

natural. But unfortunately we quickly trivialize this insight by seeking fulfillment without recognizing that in order to know and worship God rightly we must have our desires transformed. They must
be transformed — we must be trained to desire rightly — because, bent
by sin, we have little sense of what it is that we should rightly want.

A no less serious result of this kind of reductionistic theology is
the loss of a clear claim to the truth of Christian convictions. For there
is no stronger indication of the modern religious situation than that
we no longer know how or what it would mean to claim religious convictions as true. The only choice is between "fideism" — that is, that
religious convictions must be held as faith since they are not capable
of evidential challenge — or capitulation.[15] We cannot take the time
to discover all the reasons for this; however, one central reason is surely the fact that we accord to science the primary status for determining the nature of truth. Subjected to science's verification criteria,
religion appears to be merely opinion. While science cannot establish
the truth of certan hypotheses, it at least has tests for falsity. But we
are by no means sure how we can scientifically test the conviction that
God has called a people into the world to testify to the power of the
kingdom.

Some make a virtue of this difference by suggesting that religion
is different than science and technology and thus does not affect our
understanding of the scientific aspect of our world. But according to
this account, science still needs religion to show it which human
values to serve. The trouble with this strategy is that it makes the
truth value of religion merely functional.

Another challenge to questions of religious truth comes from
within religion itself. We have become increasingly aware of the
historically contingent starting point of the Christian faith. Neither
do we know the full historical "truth" about Jesus, nor does there
seem any way historically to get to that truth. Thus Gotthold Lessing's question continues to haunt us as we wonder how it is possible
to stake our life on a historically contingent starting point.[16] We feel
we should risk our lives and the lives of others only on that which is
absolutely certain. Historical "truth" simply seems too fragile to build
our life upon.

And so the circle continues. The less sure we are of the truth of
our religious convictions, the more we consider them immune from
public scrutiny. But in the process we lose what seems essential to
their being true, namely that we be willing to commend them to
others. For the necessity of witness is not accidental to Christian convictions; it is at the heart of the Christian life. Those convictions can-

not be learned except as they are attested to and exemplified by others. The essential Christian witness is neither to personal experience, nor to what Christianity means to "me," but to the truth that this world is the creation of a good God who is known through the people of Israel and the life, death, and resurrection of Jesus Christ.

Without such a witness we only abandon the world to the violence derived from the lies that devour our lives. There is, therefore, an inherent relation between truthfulness and peacefulness because peace comes only as we are transformed by a truth that gives us the confidence to rely on nothing else than its witness. A "truth" that must use violence to secure its existence cannot be truth. Rather the truth that moves the sun and the stars is that which is so sure in its power that it refuses to compel compliance or agreement by force. Rather it relies on the slow, hard, and seemingly unrewarding work of witness, a witness which it trusts to prevail even in a fragmented and violent world.

4. THE TRUTHFULNESS OF CHRISTIAN CONVICTIONS

The modern moral and religious situation I have reviewed makes the task of Christian ethics precarious at best. The temptations and pitfalls are innumerable. At a time when we are no longer sure our religious beliefs are true, perhaps the most destructive of these temptations is to salvage some significance for religion by claiming it can hold back the moral anarchy that threatens us. Calling on religion to supply those absolute values we think necessary to support the leaking breakwater of our civilization, we train "religious ethicists" to teach courses in business ethics, medical ethics, and value clarification.

But this strategy avoids the most essential question. We should not want to know if religious convictions are functional; we should want to know if they are true. Furthermore such an approach seems to imply that Christian ethics can create a morality when one is missing. Yet this is futile insofar as ethics depends upon vital communities sufficient to produce well-lived lives. If such lives do not exist, then no amount of reflection can do anything to make our ethics fecund.

We cannot assume that ethical reflection will free us from the ambiguity of living among the fragments. In fact, honest and careful ethical reflection will most likely expose more subtle difficulties for the moral actor in a fragmented world. The task of Christian ethics is not to relieve us of the ambiguity but to help us understand rightly what it means to live in the world we do—that is, to live truthfully in a world without certainty.

Finally, the absolutist strategy misconstrues the meaning and the task of Christian ethics. The task of Christian ethics is to help us see how our convictions *are* in themselves a morality. We do not first believe certain things about God, Jesus, and the church, and subsequently derive ethical implications from these beliefs. Rather our convictions embody our morality; our beliefs are our actions. We Christians ought not to search for the "behavioral implications" of our beliefs. Our moral life is not comprised of beliefs plus decisions; our moral life is the process in which our convictions form our character to be truthful.

To do justice to the way Christian convictions work, we must first develop the conceptual tools to inquire into how those convictions shape the moral life. I hope to do just this in my next chapter, with attention to narrative, vision, and character. I realize that before I try to say what specific convictions Christian ethics entail, I must first give an account of the aspects of our moral experience with which those convictions converge. This is not to say that Christian convictions ever stand apart from the moral life—we have already seen that there is no abstract account of ethics—but in our attempt to unfold the relationship we must move from one to the other. In any case, what must not be abandoned is the inherently practical nature of Christian convictions. Learning how Christian convictions are a morality is crucial for understanding what it means to claim those convictions are true. Too often religious belief is presented as a primitive mythical worldview, or metaphysics, that cannot be considered true in any verifiable sense. It is assumed that religious language describes the world only indirectly, metaphorically, or poetically.

In this book I contend that Christian convictions do not poetically soothe the anxieties of the contemporary self. Rather, they transform the self to true faith by creating a community that lives faithful to the one true God of the universe. When self and nature are thus put in right relation we perceive the truth of our existence. But because truth is unattainable without a corresponding transformation of self, "ethics," as the investigation of that transformation, does not follow after a prior systematic presentation of the Christian faith, but is *at the beginning* of Christian theological reflection.

2. A Qualified Ethic: The Narrative Character of Christian Ethics

1. THE ABSTRACTNESS OF AN UNQUALIFIED ETHIC

The first chapter suggested that there is no such thing as universal "ethics" but that every ethic requires a qualifier. Such a suggestion is deeply at odds with the main direction of modern ethical theory, which seeks a foundation for morality that will free moral judgments from their dependence on historically contingent communities. I have already identified problems in this project; here I will explore them further, focusing primarily on that project's neglect of essential aspects of our moral experience such as narrative and virtue. More importantly, I will begin to show why Christian ethics must insist on the significance of the qualifier "Christian." In contrast to the universalizing tendency, I will argue that Christian ethics reflects a particular people's history, the appropriation of which requires the recognition that we are sinners.

Modern ethical theory has underwritten, often in quite different ways, what Bernard Williams has characterized as the "midair" stance.[1] Desiring to avoid any arbitrary normative recommendation, ethicists have sought to formulate a "metaethics"—that is, a formal account of the nature and basis of moral concepts—which in itself entails no single proscriptive alternative. Such a framework is meant to undergird the nonarbitrary aspects of our actual moralities. Though sometimes criticized as vacuous, metaethical reflection has hoped to defeat any vicious subjectivism or relativism by showing that there exists a high ground which insures moral objectivity and which thus guarantees the constant capacity to "step back" from particular judgments and regard them from anyone's point of view.

However, this supposed objectivity is actually the distorted image of subjectivism. It schools us to assume we can, and perhaps always should, respond to any purported immoral action with "Who am I to say that is wrong?" As Bernard Williams points out, both the subjectivist and nonsubjectivist have no adequate justification for a response insofar as it is itself a moral thought. In mid air "it tries to stand outside all moral positions (including the thinker's own) and yet still be a moral thought. But this midair place, by subjectivism itself, is not a place in which anyone can have a moral thought" because it forces us to assume a stance external to our commitments and cares, which are the lifeblood of any morality.[2]

Such an account of objectivity has the peculiar effect of alienating the moral agent from his or her projects. It requires one always to look upon one's own projects as if they were anyone's. But by constantly "stepping back" from our projects and evaluating them from an "objective" point of view, we rob the moral life of those characteristics from which it derives its rationale — namely, the close identification of what we ought to do with what we want to be as a concrete moral agent. But we do not, nor should we, live as if we are eternally critics toward ourselves and others. Rather we must and should form our lives by our desires, wants, and cares.

Williams does not think those who wish to assume a "midair" stance are properly able to argue the question "Why should I be moral?" Ethics does not begin (nor is it required to begin) with an attempt to answer that question. A disciplined set of analytic skills, ethics begins with the recognition that we are *already* in the moral adventure. We are able to proceed, not because we share a common rationality, but because we find ourselves to be people who care about something.[3] That we care is enough to ensure intelligible conversation with anyone who thinks he or she can opt out of moral involvement.

From such a perspective the consistent amoralist does not make a rational mistake but a human mistake. As Williams points out, however, it is very difficult for the amoralist to be consistent.

> If he [the amoralist] objects (as he no doubt will) to other people treating him as he treats them, this will be perfectly consistent so long as his objecting consists just in such things as his not liking it and fighting back. What he cannot consistently do is *resent* it or disapprove of it, for these are attitudes within the moral system. . . .
>
> This illustrates, as do many of his activities, the obvious fact that this man is a parasite on the moral system, and he and his satisfactions could not exist as they do unless others operated differently. For, in general, there can be no society without some moral rules, and he needs society; also he takes more particular

advantage of moral institutions like promising and of moral dispositions of people around him.[4]

Williams's argument, while powerful, weakens with his reference to "the moral system." There is not one "moral system," but many moral systems. Moreover it is not obvious that such systems are primarily constituted by "moral rules." Indeed, with his reference to rules, Williams gives weight to the assumption that the primary focus of moral reflection should be on principles, rules, and/or promises. Emphasis on principle and rule is part of the metaethical scheme insofar as it is hoped that such rules will provide an objective, rational foundation for morality.

1.1   Rules and Obligations

Of course it can be pointed out that there is nothing odd about the emphasis on the centrality of rules for morality. Most moralities are characterized by a stress on the importance of rules, even though they may disagree about content or the scale of priority. For example, consider the process of moral education which begins by schooling the young in rules so that they may later learn to nuance and qualify them.

It is certainly not my intention to deny the significance of rules. Yet I wish to distinguish between the general existence of rules in a society and the marked emphasis upon them in modern morality and theory. Not all societies emphasize rules to the extent ours does. Aristotle seldom mentions them; and although lawlike pronouncements have a prominent place in the Scriptures, they are certainly never treated as an end in themselves or as capable of independent justification. In order to properly understand the significance of rules for our conduct, I must provide a brief analysis of the many kinds and functions of rules.

Our relatively recent fascination with rules draws on the promise they seem to hold for the impersonal justification of our moral behavior. Rules give the appearance of ensuring the objectivity we otherwise find lacking in our individual decisions and judgments. Accordingly, moral reasoning attempts to justify any particular judgment by appeal to a more universal rule or principle to which any rational creature must adhere. Thus morality is thought to acquire the unbiased quality associated, mistakenly perhaps, with legal process and therefore to secure the objectivity necessary for moral agreement.

Such a picture of the moral life fails to do justice to the variety of rules and their function in our actual morality. While rules are present in many activities, their features in one area may be lacking in another. Thus rules play a different role in games than in scientific investigation and different yet in etiquette, law, and religion. Moreover the force of some rules is quite different from others. Some rules restrict, others regulate, and still others grant permission. We view them differently if enacted by a legislative body or by custom (which changes); still others seem to be so inherent in everyday practices we never think of them as rules. Further, their scope differs. Some, we believe, apply to all (these are not necessarily the most general), while others apply only to those performing certain functions.[5]

Plato and Aristotle considered rules to be secondary to the virtues, which served to direct us to their true end, the human good. In our own day, however, questions concerning our ultimate end ("telos"), or what characterizes "the good life" have been dismissed because they are not subject to rational argument.[6] Rules in our society, therefore, are not derived from some fundamental conception of the human good. They are the basis of morality only insofar as they represent a consensus about what is necessary to ensure societal peace and survival.

As a result of the loss of a telos that would make certain rules intelligible it has seemed we can only choose between two quite different accounts of moral rules—those of Kant and the utilitarians. For Kant, rules are those requirements of action which every rational creature, regardless of his or her aims, must observe. In contrast, John Stuart Mill and the utilitarians argue that moral rules are but generalizations of our experience of what best serves to promote the greatest happiness for the greatest number. In spite of the significant differences between these positions, they share the common assumption that ethics, first and foremost, should embody an adequate theory of moral obligation derived from, or involving in a fundamental manner, rules and principles.[7] They differ only about what single principle best supports and orders our rule-determined obligations.

It has thus seemed to many philosophers that the fundamental task of ethics, given the confusion of our age, is to develop a theory sufficient to account for our primary moral obligations. A theory is needed, it seems, because it is assumed that convention, in and of itself, cannot be sufficient to determine which of our moral principles and rules are objective and nonarbitrary. The primary debate in ethics has thus hinged on whether "teleological" or "deontological" theories best account for our moral experience. Though each theory has many variations, generally the former maintains that the criteria of what is morally right or wrong is determined by consequences — that is, what produces the best balance of good over evil; the latter, on the other hand, maintains that the rightness or wrongness of certain actions are determined by the act itself — that is, the act is good or bad insofar as it is based on our duty. Thus the teleologists generally feel we ought to keep our promises because by doing so more good than evil obtains. The deontologists maintain we ought to keep our promises because by their very nature promises are meant to be kept. Teleological accounts tend to give a more secondary status to rules, therefore, than deontological theories.

Though these two positions are often depicted as antithetical, in fact they share some fundamental assumptions. Each assumes that moral philosophy gains its primary rationale from acknowledgment of some moral quandary, when, for example, there is a conflict between rules. Little attention is paid, therefore, to how or why a "situation" came to be described as a "moral" problem in the first place. Ethics, it seems, begins with questions such as "Should I or should I not have an abortion?" But then no account is given for why and how we have come to describe a certain set of circumstances as abortion, or adultery, or murder, and so on.

The concentration on "obligations" and "rules" also has the effect of distorting our moral psychology by separating our actions from our agency. Since "obligations" must be determined from the observer's standpoint, actions, it is assumed, can be characterized independently of agents, and their intentions; thus it appears that the agent's intentions are inconsequential in the moral description and evaluation of the action. To argue against this position is not to deny that communities can and do come to agree on certain prevailing descriptions of situations that school us in how we should understand our own behavior as well as that of others. At times particular agents may claim that such a description is insufficient to account for the complexity of their own situation. Such situations are but reminders of the significance of the agent's intentions for all action descriptions. Communities teach us what kind of intentions are appropriate if we are to be the kind of person appropriate to living among these people. Thus questions of what we ought to be are necessary background for questions of what we ought to do. The concentration on obligations and rules as morally primary ignores the fact that action descriptions gain their intelligibility from the role they play in a community's history and therefore for individuals in that community. When "acts" are abstracted from that history, the moral self cannot help but appear as an unconnected series of actions lacking continuity and unity.

Perhaps it is because we sense so deeply the need for unity, for integrity, that we take for granted one of the other assumptions shared by deontological and teleological theories. Each assumes that order and coherence for morality as an institution, and thus for the individual, can only be secured by establishing a single fundamental principle as a criterion from which the various rules and obligations are derived and ranked. Utilitarianism perhaps presents the clearest example of this because of the simplicity of the formula "the greatest good for the greatest number," but deontological systems often seek a similar overriding principle. Such a principle, even if it is highly formal, seems necessary since both theories assume that any apparent moral conflict must ultimately be resolved in the light of some more general principle. As a result neither theory can countenance the idea of moral tragedy—that is, the possibility of irresolvable moral conflict.

Yet we live in a world of such conflicts and we cannot negotiate that world unless we are trained with virtues sufficient to sustain us in that endeavor. But the attempt to develop an unqualified ethic, with the attending stress on rules and obligations, has resulted in a failure to stress exactly those virtues we need to live in such a world. From the perspective of an unqualified ethic it is assumed that only when we can answer the question "What ought we to do?" can we answer "What ought we to be?" While I have no wish to argue that an "ethics of virtue" must be prior to an "ethics of obligation,"[8] it is nonetheless the case that concentration on the latter has left us with too few resources to face the moral dangers of a violent world. In particular, we have failed to see that the virtues needed can only be displayed by drawing on a particular community's account of the good, and that account necessarily takes the form of a narrative.

Moreover in our concern to develop an unqualified ethic in the hope of securing peace between people of diverse beliefs and histories, we have overlooked the most important contribution that Christian convictions make for the moral life. For the accounts of an unqualified ethic make irrelevant for morality the essential Christian convictions about the nature of God and God's care of us through his calling of Israel and the life of Jesus. Our "beliefs" about such matters are relegated to some separate "religious aspects" of our lives, where they make little difference to our moral existence.

1.2   The Travail of Christian Ethics as an Unqualified Ethic

As we shall see in chapter 4, some Christian ethicists have characteristically claimed a universality very similar to that of recent philosophical ethics. They tend to presume that we have a theological stake in an adequate philosophical defense of an unqualified ethic. Yet, oddly enough, this assumption makes positive theological convictions ethically secondary. For if we know what we ought to do on grounds separate from our religious beliefs, then what are we to make morally of those theological convictions? Usually these ethicists relegate such convictions to a "higher morality" or to the "motivational" aspects of the moral life. Both alternatives entail a moral psychology which artificially severs agents and their actions; what we "ought to do" is abstracted from the question of who we are.

No less distorting for Christian ethics is the assumption that we must choose between teleological and deontological theories of obligation.[9] Of course, there are aspects of the Christian tradition that seem to fit into either theory. Those inclined toward the deontological option tend to emphasize God's commanding presence or the necessity of covenant fidelity.[10] Those more attracted to the teleological alternative often stress love as the overriding aspect of Christian ethics.[11] There is no reason to deny that the biblical record and Christian tradition manifest deontological and teleological tendencies, but it is mistaken to assume that Christian ethics requires us to choose either alternative or some combination of the two. For when we do so we inevitably tend to abstract the Christian "ethic" from its rationale by subordinating theological convictions to prior formal patterns of ethical argument.

For example, many who are convinced that ethics is primarily a matter of rules, assume that Christian ethics must have its primary source in the Ten Commandments or the Sermon on the Mount. While both are extremely significant for Christian ethical thinking, they are unintelligible when treated as sets of rules justifiable in themselves. The Decalogue is part of the covenant of God with Israel. Divorced from that covenant it makes no sense. God does indeed command obedience, but our God is the God who "brought you out of the land of Egypt, out of the house of bondage" (Deut. 5:6). Because of this action the demand "You shall have no other god before me" can be made. So too, the commands not to kill, not to commit adultery, and not to steal necessarily make sense only within the particularity of the story of God's dealing with Israel.[12] For this reason each time we receive God's commands we are reminded that:

> We were Pharaoh's slaves in Egypt; and the Lord brought us out of Egypt with a mighty hand; and the Lord showed signs and wonders, great and grievous, against Egypt and against Pharaoh

and all his household, before our eyes; and he brought us out
from there, that he might bring us in and give us the land which
he swore to give to our fathers. And the Lord commanded us
to do all these statutes, to fear the Lord our God, for our good
always, that he might preserve us alive, as at this day. And it
will be righteousness for us, if we are careful to do all this commandment before the Lord our God, as he has commanded us.
(Deut. 6:21–25)

It is no wonder that this aspect of biblical morality is ignored by
those who emphasize an ethic of obligation in the interest of developing an ahistorical ethic. For the Bible is fundamentally a story of a
people's journey with their God. A "biblical ethic" will necessarily be
one that portrays life as growth and development. In contrast, an emphasis on rule-determined obligations abstracted from this story
makes our existence appear to be only "one damn thing after
another."

We should not be surprised, then, if the kind of convictions
Christians hold are better exhibited by an analysis of the virtues. As
MacIntyre has suggested, to develop a

> stance on the virtues will be to adopt a stance on the narrative
> character of life. Why this might be so is easy to understand. If
> a human life is understood as a progress through harms and
> dangers, moral and physical, which someone may encounter
> and overcome in better and worse ways and with a greater or
> lesser measure of success, the virtues will find their place as
> those qualities the possession and exercise of which generally
> tend to success in this enterprise and the vices likewise as
> qualities which likewise tend to failure.[13]

Jews and Christians understand themselves to be in such an adventure, a journey capable of being sustained by the moral resources God
has given them. The story of this people on a journey and the place
of the virtues are inherently interwoven. I shall try to make more clear
why and how this is the case.

2. THE NARRATIVE CHARACTER OF CHRISTIAN CONVICTIONS

The nature of Christian ethics is determined by the fact that
Christian convictions take the form of a story, or perhaps better, a set
of stories that constitutes a tradition, which in turn creates and forms
a community. Christian ethics does not begin by emphasizing rules

or principles, but by calling our attention to a narrative that tells of God's dealing with creation. To be sure, it is a complex story with many different subplots and digressions, but it is crucial for us at this point in the book to see that it is not accidentally a narrative.

Too often we assume the narrative character of Christian convictions is incidental to those convictions. Both believer and unbeliever are under the impression that narrative is a relatively unimportant moral category. Specifically, we tend to think of "stories" as illustrations of some deeper truth that we can and should learn to articulate in a non-narrative mode. Thus, when we are children we make do with stories, but when we grow up we want the literal truth — that is, the truth that can be substantiated apart from the story. Augustus Compte even suggested that such a development corresponds to the history of the race, noting that we have now reached the age of science, in which we no longer have the need for stories (myths). Ironically, Compte failed to notice that he told a story to show we have now reached the age in which we no longer require stories!

Moreover we naturally associate stories and narratives with fiction. Stories create a fantasy world that releases us from the burden of having to deal with the real world. The stories of God in Scripture, it is thought, are but attempts to say "mythically" or "symbolically" what might be said directly, but because of the nature of the object being described can only be reached through "poetic" form. Such stories of God, like most stories, are perhaps important to comfort us, but one is mistaken to ask if they are true.

I think this is a dire misreading of the narrative character of Christian convictions. My contention is that the narrative mode is neither incidental nor accidental to Christian belief. There is no more fundamental way to talk of God than in a story.[14] The fact that we come to know God through the recounting of the story of Israel and the life of Jesus is decisive for our truthful understanding of the kind of God we worship as well as the world in which we exist. Put directly, the narrative character of our knowledge of God, the self, and the world is a reality-making claim that the world and our existence in it are God's creations; our lives, and indeed, the existence of the universe are but contingent realities.

Some may think that emphasis on narrative as the primary grammar of Christian belief is a theological mistake. Surely we can talk about God in a more fundamental manner than through stories — e.g., through doctrine. Doctrinally we affirm that God is our creator and/or redeemer, or that God's essential nature is that of a trinitarian relationship. But such emphasis ignores the fact that such "doctrines" are themselves a story, or perhaps better, the outline of the story.[15] Claims such as "God is creator" are simply shorthand ways of reminding us that we believe we are participants in a much more elaborate story, of which God is the author. Doctrines, therefore, are not the upshot of the stories; they are not the meaning or heart of the stories. Rather they are tools (sometimes even misleading tools), meant to help us tell the story better. Because the Christian story is an enacted story, liturgy is probably a much more important resource than are doctrines or creeds for helping us to hear, tell, and live the story of God.

Narrative is not secondary for our knowledge of God; there is no "point" that can be separated from the story. The narratives through which we learn of God *are* the point. Stories are not substitute explanations we can someday hope to supplant with more straightforward accounts. Precisely to the contrary, narratives are necessary to our understanding of those aspects of our existence which admit of no further explanation—i.e., God, the world, and the self.

Actually it is not incidental that knowledge of God, the world, and the self seem to have similar epistemological status. On analysis each appears a strange "object," since it seems that our knowledge of one is dependent on the other. To "know" God requires a rethinking of what and how we know the self and the world. To know one's self, one cannot but make claims about the kind of world in which selves are able to exist. Neither God, the world, nor the self are properly known as separate entities but are in a relation requiring concrete display. That display takes the form of a narrative in which we discover that the only way to "know" God, the world, or the self is through their history.

Narrative plays a larger part in our lives than we often imagine. For example, we frequently introduce ourselves through narrative. To be sure, any story with which we identify "ourselves" can be and should be constantly tested by the history we have lived. But the telling of the narrative is itself a reinterpretation of the history. We see that because the self is historically formed we require a narrative to speak about it if we are to speak at all. One should not think of oneself as exemplifying or being some individual instance of a self, but one understands in what his or her selfhood consists only insofar as he or she learns to tell that particular story.

Just as narrative is a crucial category for the knowledge of the self, so it is for our knowledge of God. "God," we must remember, is a common name, to which we can ascribe attributions only as we learn of God through a history. This, of course, follows from the basic theological claim that knowledge of God and knowledge of the self are interdependent. But once the formal nature of this claim is fleshed out in terms of narrative, we see its implications for the Christian life. Not only is knowledge of self tied to knowledge of God, but we know ourselves truthfully only when we know ourselves in relation to God. We know who we are only when we can place our selves — locate our stories — within God's story.

This is the basis for the extraordinary Christian claim that we participate morally in God's life. For our God is a God who wills to include us within his life. This is what we mean when we say, in shorthand as it were, that God is a God of grace. Such shorthand can be dangerous if it is mistaken for the suggestion that our relationship with God has an immediacy that makes the journey of the self with God irrelevant. Grace is not an eternal moment above history rendering history irrelevant; rather it is God's choice to be a Lord whose kingdom is furthered by our concrete obedience through which we acquire a history befitting our nature as God's creatures.

To learn to be God's creatures means we must learn to recognize that our existence and the existence of the universe itself is a gift. It is a gift that God wills to have our lives contribute to the eschatological purposes for creation. As creatures we cannot hope to return to God a gift of such magnitude. But we can respond with a willingness to receive. To learn to be God's creature, to accept the gift, is to learn to be at home in God's world. Just as we seek to make a guest feel "at home" in our home, so God seeks to have us feel "at home" by providing us with the opportunity to appropriate the gift in the terms it was given — that is, gratuitously.[16]

The impossibility of reciprocity for God's gift is not without analogies in our common experience. We cannot return our parent's love except as we receive it and love others similarly. Also each of us are recipients of favors strewn through our lives. Some are given anonymously; others we do not even notice. As Kenneth Schmitz notes, "I cannot make use of the simplest technique which did not have to be discovered and brought to excellence by nameless craftsmen; so that most of my benefactors remain unknown to me. Some of us can name a few generations of our ancestors, but before long the chain of those who have helped to give us life fades away into obscurity."[17] Indeed, to gratefully inherit a tradition is but to recognize and honor the chain of actual benefactors who have sustained the skills and stories that provide us with the means to know and live our lives as God's creatures.

Christians and Jews are traditioned people who believe that they have been invited to share a particular history that reflects the God who has brought us into being. To know our creator, therefore, we are required to learn through God's particular dealings with Israel and Jesus, and through God's continuing faithfulness to the Jews and the ingathering of a people to the church. Such knowledge requires constant appropriation, constant willingness to accept the gift of God's good creation. As Christians we maintain that such appropriation is accomplished in and through our faithfulness to the life, death, and resurrection of Jesus. We believe that by learning to be his disciples we will learn to find our life — our story — in God's story. In the process we find our life in relation to other lives; we discover that as Christians our lives are intelligible only as we acknowledge indebtedness to the people of Israel, both in the past and in their continued presence.

To sum up, the emphasis on narrative as theologically central for an explication of Christian existence reminds us of at least three crucial claims.[18] First, narrative formally displays our existence and that of the world as creatures — as *contingent* beings. Narrative is required precisely because the world and events in the world do not exist by necessity. Any attempt to depict our world and ourselves nonnarratively is doomed to failure insofar as it denies our contingent nature. Correlatively, narrative is epistemically fundamental for our knowledge of God and ourselves, since we come to know ourselves only in God's life.

Second, narrative is the characteristic form of our awareness of ourselves as *historical* beings who must give an account of the purposive relation between temporally discrete realities. Indeed, the ability to provide such an account, to sustain its growth in a living tradition, is the central criterion for identifying a group of people as a community. Community joins us with others to further the growth of a tradition whose manifold storylines are meant to help individuals identify and navigate the path to the good. The self is subordinate to the community rather than vice versa, for we discover the self through a community's narrated tradition.

From this it can be understood why the stress on narrative is a correlative to the claim that every ethic requires a qualifier. No ethic can be freed from its narrative, and thus communal, context. To the extent that practical reason seeks to avoid its inherent historical character, it relinquishes any power to enable us to order our lives in accordance with our true ends. We thus become alienated from ourselves; we lose the ability to locate the history of which we are a part.

Third, God has revealed himself narratively in the history of

Israel and in the life of Jesus. While much of Scripture does not take narrative literary form, it is perhaps not incidental that the Gospels do.[19] In any case, Scripture as a whole tells the story of the covenant with Israel, the life, death, and resurrection of Jesus, and the ongoing history of the church as the recapitulation of that life. This empirical observation is not merely an interesting one; this notion of the essential nature of *narrative as the form of God's salvation* is why we rightly attribute to Scripture the truth necessary for our salvation.[20]

Of course, we cannot be brought to understanding without training, for we resist at least the part of the narrative which describes us as sinful creatures. We can only know God by having our lives transformed through initiation into the kingdom. Such a transformation requires that we see the world as it is, not as we want it to be — that is, as sinful and ourselves as sinners. Thus the story requires transformation as it challenges the presumption of our righteousness and teaches us why we so badly need to be reborn through the baptism offered by this new community.

2.1   Narrative as a Reality-making Claim

As I have tried to show, emphasis on narrative is not an attempt to beg the question of the truthfulness of Christian convictions by turning them into a provocative account of human existence. On the contrary, attention to the narrative character of God's activity and our life reveals the nature of reality. Since our existence is historically determined, we should not be surprised to discover that our moralities are historical; they require a qualifier. We are unable to stand outside our histories in midair, as it were; we are destined to discover ourselves only within God's history, for God is our beginning and our end.

Christian ethics, therefore, is not first of all concerned with "Thou shalt" or "Thou shalt not." Its first task is to help us rightly envision the world. Christian ethics is specifically formed by a very definite story with determinative content. If we somehow discover the world is not as that story suggests, then we have good grounds for not believing in, or more accurately, not worshipping the God revealed in the life, cross, and resurrection of Jesus. In other words, the enterprise of Christian ethics primarily helps us to see. We can only act within the world we can envision, and we can envision the world rightly only as we are trained to see. We do not come to see merely by looking, but must develop disciplined skills through initiation into that community that attempts to live faithful to the story of God. Furthermore, we cannot see the world rightly unless we are changed, for as sinners we do not desire to see truthfully. Therefore Christian ethics must assert that by learning to be faithful disciples, we are more able to see the world as it is, namely God's creation.

But Christians must learn that the world, in spite of God's good creation, is also in fundamental rebellion. Such rebellion includes humanity, but is not limited to it. The revolt reaches to every aspect of our existence, since through humanity's sin all of creation has been thrown out of joint. Any suggestion that the world is sinful cannot be limited to "moralistic" claims about our petty crimes. The Christian story trains us to see that in most of our life we act as if this is not God's world and therein lies our fundamental sin. Moreover, when we so act, we find that our actions have far-reaching consequences, since in effect we distort our own and the world's nature. Therefore sin implies not just a claim about human behavior but a claim about the way things are.

That our existence is sinful adds new perspective to the claim that we must be transformed if we are to see the world truthfully. The new vision afforded us in such a transformation includes the appropriation of a truthful language. If we can see, so we can speak. That does not mean that we do not observe things we sometimes do not know how to describe, but that our *learning* to see them and our ability to interpret and share our vision with others depends on having a language appropriate to what we have seen.

Christian convictions constitute a narrative, a language, that requires a transformation of the self if we are to see, as well as be, truthful. The gospel commands us to submit to a vigorous and continuing discipleship if we are to recognize our status as subjects and properly understand the requirements for participation in the kingdom. Furthermore, to be a Christian is not principally to obey certain commandments or rules, but to learn to grow into the story of Jesus as the form of God's kingdom. We express that by saying we must learn to be disciples; only as such can we understand why at the center of creation is a cross and resurrection.

2.2   On Learning to Be a Sinner

Our lesson is most disconcerting when the narrative asks us to understand ourselves not only as friends of the crucified, but as the crucifiers. We must be trained to see ourselves as sinners, for it is not self-evident. Indeed, our sin is so fundamental that we must be taught to recognize it; we cannot perceive its radical nature so long as we remain formed by it. Sin is not some universal tendency of humankind to be inhumane or immoral, though sin may involve inhumanity and immorality. We are not sinful because we participate in some general human condition, but because we deceive ourselves about the nature of reality and so would crucify the very one who calls us to God's kingdom.

We only learn what our sin is as we discover our true identity through locating the self in God's life as revealed to us through the life, death, and resurrection of Jesus Christ. Only when we recognize ourselves as sinners of this kind can we receive the redemption that comes with assurance that because we have beheld God's glory in the cross of Jesus, our perception of ourselves as sinners will not destroy us.

The story Christians tell of God exposes the unwelcome fact that I am a sinner. For without such a narrative the fact and nature of my sin cannot help but remain hidden in self-deception. Only a narrative that helps me place myself as a creature of a gracious God can provide the skills to help me locate my sin as fundamentally infidelity and rebellion. As a creature I have been created for loyalty — loyalty to the truth, to the love that moves the sun and the stars and yet is found on a cross — but I find myself serving any powers but the true one in the hopes of being my own lord. The ironic result is that by seeking to possess I become possessed.

Christian tradition has at various times and places characterized this fundamental sin in quite different ways. Our basic sin has been said to be pride, self-love, infidelity, lust, sloth, all of which have some claim to the doubtful honor of being the father of all sins. I doubt, however, whether there is any one term sufficient to suggest the complex nature of our sin. That is exactly why we see we need the set of stories we find in Scripture and displayed by the church to recognize our sin. As narrative-determined creatures we must learn to locate our lives in God's life if we are to have the means to face, as well as do something about, our infidelity and rebellion against our true creator.

Just to the extent I refuse to be faithful to God's way, to live as part of God's life, my life assumes the character of rebellion. Our sin is not merely an error in overestimating our capacities. Rather it is the active and willful attempt to overreach our powers. It is the attempt to live *sui generis*, to live as if we are or can be the authors of our own stories. Our sin is, thus, a challenge to God's authorship and a denial that we are characters in the drama of the kingdom.

No one has better characterized this rebellion than Reinhold

Niebuhr. Niebuhr saw that sin results from our inability to live as creatures — as contingent. Our unwillingness to face our contingency breeds insecurity which we seek to overcome by a

> will-to-power which overreaches the limits of human creature-liness. Man is ignorant and involved in the limitations of a finite mind; but he pretends that he is not limited. He assumes that he can gradually transcend finite limitations until his mind becomes identical with universal mind. All of his intellectual and cultural pursuits, therefore, become infected with the sin of pride. Man's pride and will-to-power disturb the harmony of creation. The Bible defines sin in both religious and moral terms. The religious dimension of sin is man's rebellion against God, his effort to usurp the place of God. The moral and social dimension of sin is injustice. The ego which falsely makes itself the centre of existence in its pride and will-to-power inevitably subordinates other life to its will and thus does injustice to other life.
>
> Sometimes man seeks to solve the problem of the contradiction of finiteness and freedom, not by seeking to hide his finiteness and comprehending the world into himself, but by seeking to hide his freedom and by losing himself in some aspect of the world's vitalities. In that case his sin may be defined as sensuality rather than pride. Sensuality is never the mere expression of natural impulse in man. It always betrays some aspect of his abortive effort to solve the problem of finiteness and freedom. Human passions are always characterized by unlimited and demonic potencies of which animal life is innocent.[21]

While this brief quotation cannot do justice to the intricacy of Niebuhr's extraordinary analysis of the relation between pride and sensuality, it is sufficient to suggest that both result in distortion of our existence. Moreover, we live a lie when we tell a false and deceitful story about ourselves and others. Indeed, we conspire deceitfully to make our lies more powerful by structuring them so as to command consensus. The resulting "objectivity" of the majority makes our deception all the more destructive because it allows us to assume that those who challenge our consensus are not only wrong but immoral. It is not far, then, to the use of force in defense of what we think to be the truth, so our sin becomes the root and branch of violence.

If this is not a comprehensive account of sin, it is at least enough to make the point that seeing the world as sinful already includes a moral claim about reality, a claim about how the self should be situated in the world to understand properly the nature of its existence. Ethics, as we have said, is not primarily about rules and principles, rather it is about how the self must be transformed to see the world truthfully. For Christians, such seeing develops through schooling in a narrative which teaches us how to use the language of sin not only about others but about ourselves.

Of course, Christians are not just asked to see themselves as sinners. We are to do something about our sin. We are called to be disciples and even to count ourselves among the righteous. Our call is not a general admonition to be good, but a concrete and definite call to take up the way of life made possible by God's redemptive action for us in the cross. To be redeemed, as I suggested above, is nothing less than to learn to place ourselves in God's history, to be part of God's people. To locate ourselves within that history and people does not mean we must have some special experience of personal salvation. Redemption, rather, is a change in which we accept the invitation to become part of God's kingdom, a kingdom through which we acquire a character befitting one who has heard God's call. Now an intense personal experience may be important for many, but such experiences cannot in themselves be substitutes for learning to find the significance of our lives only in God's ongoing journey with creation.

We Christians locate our lives in relation to the history of a people. The gospel is not a "truth" or philosophical theory that can be appropriated by an individual in the hope of giving some meaning to his or her life. On the contrary, we find ourselves part of a community with a very particular kind of citizenship. As citizens our self-understanding may change, but this occurs only as we acquire the virtues necessary to sustain a community of peaceable people through history. Likewise, Christian ethics must serve and be formed by the Christian community, a community whose interest lies in the formation of character and whose perduring history provides the continuity we need to act in conformity with that character.

I will say more about the nature and importance of character later. However, in this context it is sufficient to note that Christian ethics is concerned more with who we are than what we do. This is not to suggest that our actions, decisions and choices are unimportant, but rather that the church has a stake in holding together our being and behaving in such a manner that our doing only can be a reflection of our character. The ongoing history of the church requires persons—characters, if you will—who are capable of living appropriate to God's activity in the life and death of Jesus Christ.

To return to an earlier point, we can now see that the insistence on the qualifier in Christian ethics is not just of formal use but is required by the material content of our convictions. That those convictions take the form of narrative and are displayed ethically by a certain character and/or particular virtues means that Christians cannot pretend to do ethics for anyone. Yet that does not mean Christian convictions are of significance only for the church, for Christians claim that by learning to find our lives within the story of God we learn to see the world truthfully. Christians must attempt to be nothing less than a people whose ethic shines as a beacon to others illumining how life should be lived well.

3. On Being Historic: Agency, Character, and Sin

1. ON BEING RESPONSIBLE FOR OUR CHARACTER

I have repeatedly stressed that there is no neutral starting point from which reflection on the nature of the moral life can begin. Christian ethics, though it claims truthfulness and therefore a certain universality, must begin and end by taking seriously the qualifier "Christian." It cannot avoid beginning with affirmations about God made by a specific community in this time and place. Christians claim such affirmations are true and objective in that they give us the skills rightly to see and act in the world, not as we want it to be, but as it is, namely, as God's good but fallen creation.

But part of what it means to recognize the world as it is, rather than as we want it to be, is to see that all existence, and in particular the human self, is narratively formed. Put differently, it is our nature to be historic beings. Reflection upon the historic, and therefore narrative, character of our existence is an enterprise integral to understanding what it means to claim as true the story Christians tell of God. For we must show that in fact our existence, our nature, corresponds to that story—namely, that we are beings whose life requires narrative display.

In the classical tradition, being human means standing between nature and spirit, between finite limits and infinite possibilities. Our ability to be spirit—that is, to be more than our physical or biological nature—is exactly what is necessary for us to be historic. But it is also the case that we cannot be historic without our physical and biological nature. It is because nature anchors us so resolutely in the concrete that we are actors capable of forming a history.[1]

But what does it mean to be capable of forming a history? It certainly does not mean that we must be able to shape "history" in the grand sense—that is, to make a mark that cannot be ignored by our descendants (although, as we shall see in our discussion of sin, we often assume that our existence *does* depend on making such a mark). To be historic means, rather, that I must be able to make my past my own. I must learn to say, "I did that." To be historic means that I must be capable of making a succession of "events" a narrative — not just any narrative, but a narrative that is sufficient to give me a sense of self, one which looks not only to my past but points to the future, thereby giving my life a telos and direction.

Yet this emphasis on the historic character of our existence seems to qualify in a decisive way what many assume is essential to our status as free beings. In their view our ability to be historic depends on our first having a freedom that always, at least in principle, guarantees our ability to step back from our engagements and thus is prior to our history. My insistence that our historic nature is prior to our being free seems to rule out the freedom necessary to claim our history as our own.

In this respect it is significant that we associate and often confuse two different senses of being historic. When we say we are "historic" we sometimes mean that we are the "products" of history. That is, we are determined by our biology, by our biographical context, by accidents of birth, by the time and place in which we grew up, and by our own past. We are what we have been made to be. But at other times we mean that we are capable of interpreting and forming our history; that by our own decisions we can take the "givens" of our life and shape them to take on the character of our wishes and desires.

To be historic involves both of these meanings, although it is not easy to see how they can both be true. Just to the extent that we are *products* of history it seems that we are thwarted, or at least severely restricted, in our attempt to *make* history. For example, when we look back over our lives many of the things we thought we were *doing* at the time now appear to have been *done* to us. Retrospectively, our own "decisions" seem more determined than manifestations of our freedom.

Even a momentous decision like deciding to marry, which I assumed to be clearly my decision at the time, appears later to have been an event that has happened to me. At the time of marrying it seemed I was making all kinds of decisions — who, when, how it would affect other plans — but as I look back on these "decisions" I cannot remember any that I can claim were fully "mine." Indeed I suspect that this is true of most "important" decisions, such as what profession we enter and where we settle. We always feel that if we had just known more at the time we would have made a better decision and been less determined. This feeling often leads to what I regard as the most basic modern deception, namely that to be free means not to be held to those "decisions" I made in the past which were less than fully mine.

One of the assumptions behind this view of freedom is the idea that the greater our awareness, the greater our freedom. Thus, the more I understand my situation, the more I know about the long-term effects of my decision, the more likely it is that I will make a free and non-determined decision that I can gladly claim as "mine" in the future. But it is by no means clear that awareness brings freedom. While it is not a decisive objection to this notion, the very fact that those who are most "aware" are often least capable of action should at least make us think twice about the notion's validity. Joseph Conrad's fiction, for example, is full of people who, because they see too much, are rendered incapable of action, and when they finally act they often do the worst possible thing.[2]

In what follows, I will try to provide an alternative account of freedom without the assumption that freedom depends primarily on the extent of our awareness of what we are doing. Rather, I will argue that freedom is a quality that derives from having a well-formed character. Put in traditional terms, only the truly good person can be the truly free person. In this view, freedom follows from courage and the ability to respond to a truthful story.

2. CHARACTER AND FREEDOM

In order to make these claims intelligible I must try to explain in more detail what I mean by character and why it is the source of our freedom. We usually associate freedom with actions, not character. We assume that the question of whether we are to be held accountable for a certain action depends on whether there were any external or internal impediments preventing us from doing what we wanted or felt we needed to do. We are concerned with impediments because we feel we can be held responsible for our actions only if they are something we have done. Put simply, we assume that only if we have a choice are we free.

Dissenting from such a view, Frithjof Bergmann has argued that to say someone has a choice says little about the whole nexus of constraints operating in a situation, or about the totality of factors that were beyond one's control.[3] To use an extreme example, I may be free to choose to die by starvation or torture, but that is hardly to be free. Of course most cases are more complex. For example, I have a friend

What is crucial to human beings as characters in enacted narratives is that, possessing only the resources of psychological continuity, we have to be able to respond to the imputation of strict identity. I am forever whatever I have been at any time for others—and I may at any time be called upon to answer for it—no matter how changed I may be now. There is no way of *founding* my identity—or lack of it—on the psychological continuity or discontinuity of the self. The self inhabits a character whose unity is given as the unity of a character.[7]

In my accounts, agency but names our ability to inhabit our character.

This understanding of agency is in stark contrast to those which would try to anchor our "freedom" in a transcendental self. For example, Timothy O'Connell defends what he calls an "onion peel view of the self." He asks us to think of persons as analogous to onions—that is, as comprised of layers. No layer stands by itself, but each has its own identity.

At the outermost layer, as it were, we find their environment, their world, the things they own. Moving inward we find their actions, their behavior, the things they do. And then the body, that which is the "belonging" of a person and yet also *is* the person. Going deeper we discover moods, emotions, feelings. Deeper still are convictions by which they define themselves. And at the very center, in that dimensionless pinpoint around which everything else revolves, is the person himself or herself—the I.[8]

O'Connell notes that this "I," this dimensionless pinpoint, cannot be an object, since if it were it would need another subject to know it as object. He suggests this mysterious entity must be the "condition of the possibility" of all we consider.[9] Thus he concludes that as agents, as doers, we are changeable, but as "be-ers," as subjects, we must necessarily stay the same.[10] If such is not the case, then there exists no guarantee that we are not simply the product, a complex product to be sure, of our biology, environment, and particular biographical situation.

According to O'Connell, our freedom can only be grounded in the fact that "we experience ourselves as men and women who are free, not only as agents but also as persons." This latter,

central core of myself, the "I" which is my personhood, is confronted with a reality that transcends all categories. It is confronted with the reality of my world, my situation, by body, my feelings, my attitudes and prejudices. In fact it is confronted even by the condition of the possibility of that reality: namely, God. And from the perspective of my own core, the subjectivity that I am, this cosmically inclusive objectivity presents itself for decision. A simple, singular decision: yes or no. The freedom of the human person, then, is not categorical freedom at all. Rather it is a freedom that transcends all categories, it is "transcendental freedom."[11]

O'Connell is never clear, however, on the relation between this "transcendental freedom" and "categorical freedom." One begins to suspect that this distinction involves all the virtues and problems of Kant's distinction between the noumenal and phenomenal worlds. O'Connell says "the cosmic exercise of transcendental freedom occurs only in and through the exercises of categorical freedom,"[12] but it is not clear what he means by that. It seems that we cannot be what we do (or do not do) — for if we are what we do, then we are not free. In order to be free we must always have an "I" that somehow stands behind what we do, an "I" not determined or affected by what we do.

From O'Connell's perspective, and I might add it is shared by many, our real identity is not our history, but the "fundamental stance" or "option" — that is, a stance by which we exercise that transcending kind of freedom in order to define ourselves as persons.[13] This seems to imply that fundamental option is but the name given to the *moment* in which that stance is assumed or emphatically renewed. It is that deeper meaning and significance some of the decisions we make in our lives seem to have. But, ironically, such a "moment" cannot be "in history," as its power lies exactly in its ability to transcend history.

One cannot help but be sympathetic to the kind of problem to which O'Connell speaks in his language of "fundamental option," but this view results in a distorted account of the self that is conceptually confusing. For example, O'Connell says that the "fundamental option" is not really something we "do"; rather it is the term we use to describe what is "really going on" within the rich activity of our lives.[14] Why, then, is it called an *option?*

Given the difficulty of crediting an account of our sense that we are not simply the sum of what has happened to us or what we have done, the language of agency is of considerable help. For to say that we are agents is an attempt to avoid transcendental appeals while rightly claiming that we have the power to be one thing rather than another, in short, to be persons of character. There is no way, however, to guarantee agency metaphysically, the way O'Connell tries to guarantee his fundamental option. Appeals to the irreplaceability of first-person avowals cannot "prove" we must be agents; such arguments can only show that attempts to deny agency involve extraordinary language-transforming proposals.

Nor do I think that the distinction between what we do and what happens to us is decisive for establishing the possibility of our agency. This is particularly the case if we must allow, as Outka suggests, that our very doing often includes—perhaps even depends upon—what has happened to us. However, the distinction between what I do and what happens to me is still important insofar as it calls attention to the inevitability of describing behavior intentionally. The language of agency reminds us that our behavior cannot be satisfactorily analyzed in terms of inanimate behavior. That is, any attempt to describe human behavior completely in terms of random causation—causally relating our actions as one random event to another—is doomed to failure. Although such descriptions cannot be shown in principle to be false, what we see is that, exactly to the extent they are intelligible, they all implicitly employ purposive and intentional categories.[15]

In terms of the account I have tried to develop to be an agent means I am able to locate my action within an ongoing history and within a community of language users. Even what has happened to me, my habit of dependency, becomes mine to the extent that I am able to make it part of my story. I am not an agent because I can "cause" certain things to happen, but because certain things that happen, whether through the result of my decision or not, can be made mine through my power of attention and intention. The "causation" proper to agents and their actions is not rendered by cause and effect, but by the agent's power of description. My act is not something I cause, as though it were external to me, but it is mine because I am able to "fit" it into my ongoing story. My power as an agent is therefore relative to the power of my descriptive ability. Yet that very ability is fundamentally a social skill, for we learn to describe through appropriating the narratives of the communities in which we find ourselves.

It is crucial to note, however, that the power of description that a narrative provides is not to be understood only as an intellectual skill. For "description," while often verbal, is just as importantly a matter of habit—indeed most verbal skills are also habits. That is why our freedom is literally carried by a community that sustains us in the habits of self-possession—not the least of which is learning to depend on and trust in others. Thus our freedom is not correlative to our self-awareness; rather it depends on the kind of habits we have acquired that are only occasionally brought to awareness. For example, the refusal to use violence for resolving disputes, or perhaps better, the attempt to avoid persistent violent situations, becomes for some so routine they never think about it. It is simply "who they are." But the formation of that habit does not make it any less, but all the more, a resource of and for their freedom.

Appeals to agency as a characteristic of the self cannot in principle guarantee our "freedom" from all determination, since our very ability to know what we have done and to claim our behavior as our own is dependent on the descriptions we learn. There is no contradiction between claims of agency and our sociality, since the extent and power of any agency depends exactly on the adequacy of the descriptions we learn from our communities. Our "freedom," therefore, is dependent on our being initiated into a truthful narrative, as in fact it is the resource from which we derive the power to "have character" at all. Put simply, our ability to "have character" does not require the positing of a transcendental freedom, rather it demands a recognition of the narrative nature of our existence. The fundamental category for ensuring agency, therefore, is not freedom but narrative.

Outka is probably quite right to suggest that some of us may be more "psychologically determined" than others. I know of no satisfactory way to assess degrees in that matter. I wonder, sometimes, if the language of "psychologically determined" is not more determining than the supposed dependency itself. However, the crucial point is that claims of agency are not meant to guarantee absolute freedom or independence. Freedom, or agency, is not a name for some real or ideal state in which we have absolute control of our lives. Rather "agency" is but the word we use to remind us that we are beings who have the capacity to claim our lives by learning to grow in a truthful narrative. Such a capacity is not guaranteed by our having a "truer" self than our character. For our character is exactly that which grants us freedom, as it is constituted by those skills of description which allow us to make both what we have done and what has happened to us part of an ongoing narrative.

Such skills are not just "intellectual" but also moral. To face our lives truthfully requires trust and courage, for if we are to be free we must learn to see what we have done without illusion and deception. So the formation of courage is even greater than the power of choice, as we must be trained to face our destiny of death, not with denial, but with hope. Short of such courage no amount of transcendental freedom or fundamental option can provide the necessary basis for our ability to make our lives our own.

3. FREEDOM AS THE PRESENCE OF THE OTHER

But it may still be objected that some people's capacity for agency, their ability to respond to a truthful story, is so buried by accidents of their history, so crippled by their past, or so determined by a story that has taught them to despise themselves, that they have lost (or never found) the ability to participate in the forming of their character. More plausibly, their lives are so complex, their responses shaped by so many different stories, that the unity of character which seems necessary to order the multiplicity of loyalties in their lives may well seem unattainable.[16]

No guarantee can be given to insure any one person from being so "determined." Yet it is the Christian claim that no one is so completely determined that he or she lacks all means to respond to the story of God and thus find some means to make his life his own. Such a claim is not based on optimistic assumptions about our goodness or our innate ability. Rather it is an affirmation of God's unrelenting desire to have each of us serve in the kingdom. The call to such service we find only in the presence of another, whose need is often the very occasion of our freedom. For it is through the need of another that the greatest hindrance to my freedom, namely my own self-absorption, is finally not so much overcome as simply rendered irrelevant. It is through the other that I am finally able to make peace with myself and thus have the power to make my life my own.

As Christians we believe that peace is most perfectly realized as we learn to find our role in God's story. That is, the peremptory story of peace as peace, the sense of being at home, comes only as we learn to live true to our nature as God's creatures. Moreover God has charged us with the particular responsibility of being his representatives to attract others to that story of peace by manifesting it in our common life. That is why Christians feel such an urgency to witness, to offer the stranger hospitality, so that God's peace might be possessed by all.

It is the privilege of Christians, as well as their responsibility, to tell God's story to those who know it not. But "to tell God's story" is to put the matter far too simply. For God's story is not merely told; it must be lived. We do not respond to the story simply in itself, rather the story grasps our attention through the form of another person. The "freedom" provided by that narrative thus comes only in the form of someone external to me; it must come in the presence of another. I am an agent just to the extent I have the capacity to be called from myself by another.

We acquire character through the expectations of others. The "otherness" of another's character not only invites me to an always imperfect imitation, but challenges me to recognize the way my vision is restricted by my own self-preoccupation. Thus the kind of community in which we encounter another does not merely make *some* difference for our capacity for agency, it makes *all* the difference. From this perspective we are not the creators of our character; rather, our character is a gift from others which we learn to claim as our own by recognizing it as a gift. Our freedom is literally in the hands of others. I am free just to the extent that I can trust others to stand over against me and call my own "achievements" into question. It is from them that I learn the story that gives my life a purpose and direction.

Our ability to have character and our capacity to recognize our existence as a gift go hand in hand. The narrative that provides us with character is not one that depicts one clear end that we must pursue at the cost of all others. Rather it is a story that we must continually learn from the presence of others as we learn through them and their pursuits better to understand what it is we are pursuing. To be sure, some sense of the telos of the narrative is needed to set us on our way, but, as MacIntyre reminds us, such a quest is "not at all that of a search for something already adequately characterised, as miners search for gold or geologists for oil. It is in the course of the quest and only through encountering and coping with the various particular harms, dangers, temptations and distractions which provide any quest with its episodes and incidents that the goal of the quest is finally to be understood. A quest is always an education both as to the character of that which is sought and in self-knowledge."[17]

Our initiation into a story as well as the ability to sustain ourselves in that story depends on others who have gone before and those who continue to travel with us. "What I am, therefore, is in key part what I inherit, a specific past that is present to some degree in my present. I find myself part of a history and that is generally to say, whether I like it or not, whether I recognise it or not, one of the bearers of a tradition."[18] Given this, the crucial question becomes whether the tradition is more or less truthful. At least one of the conditions of a truthful tradition is its own recognition that it is not final, that it needs to grow and change if it is to adequately shape our futures in a faithful manner. For, again, as MacIntyre suggests,

A living tradition . . . is an historically extended, socially embodied argument, and an argument precisely in part about the
goods which constitute that tradition. Within a tradition the pursuit of goods extends through generations, sometimes through
many generations. Hence the individual's search for his or her
good is generally and characteristically conducted within a context defined by those traditions of which the individual's life is
a part.[19]

The Christian tradition holds us accountable, not to an abstract
story, but to a body of people who have been formed by the life of
Jesus. By learning to make his life our life we see we are free just to
the extent that we learn to trust others and make ourselves available
to be trusted by others. Such trust is possible because the story of his
life, by the very way we learn it, requires that we recognize and accept
the giftedness of our existence: I did not create myself but what I am
has been made possible by others. Our dependence on others, of
course, has as much potential for evil as it does for good—that is exactly why the gospel is so remarkable, as it requires that we transform
our distrust to trust on the basis of our knowledge and experience
that God's providence is working in all our trusts and distrusts.[20]

God is not necessary, therefore, to ensure the existence of a transcendental "I," nor is God but a correlate to such an "I." Rather God
is the ultimate given whom we can confidently trust as the basis of
our freedom. By becoming a part of the people who carry the story
of Jesus, we are initiated into an adventure through which we learn
the disciplines and virtues necessary to make our lives our own. For
to continue that story, the life of Christ, is the source of our freedom.
We are finally no self, no agent, until we are the self that God has
called us to be.

4. OUR SINFUL CHARACTER

The recognition that we are most free when we are formed by
a story that helps us live appropriate to the reality that our life is a
gift is also the context for rightly understanding what it means to be
a sinner. Earlier I suggested that sin is not a natural category, that we
have to be taught we are sinners. Moreover sin is not just an error or
the doing of certain prohibited actions, but sin is the positive attempt
to overreach our power as creatures. It is manifested in our pride and
sensuality, but its fundamental form is self-deception.

We are now in a position to develop this understanding of sin further, for we can see that the very claim of freedom as a possession, as our achievement, is but a manifestation of our sin. We are rooted in sin just to the extent we think we have the inherent power to claim our life—our character—as our particular achievement. In other words, our sin—our fundamental sin—is the assumption that we are the creators of the history through which we acquire and possess our character. Sin is the form our character takes as a result of our fear that we will be "nobody" if we lose control of our lives.

Moreover our need to be in control is the basis for the violence of our lives. For since our "control" and "power" cannot help but be built on an insufficient basis, we must use force to maintain the illusion that we are in control. We are deeply afraid of losing what unity of self we have achieved. Any idea or person threatening that unity must be either manipulated or eliminated. We fear others because they always stand as an implicit challenge to our deceptions. Thus it seems the inherent necessity of all people to have or create an enemy.

This helps us understand why we are so resistant to the training offered by the gospel, for we simply cannot believe that the self might be formed without fear of the other. Such a formation of course is indeed extraordinary, for it is only possible if in fact we receive our true self from God. There has always been something right about the traditional understanding that the unity of the self and the knowledge of God are correlates. Such a unity does not come automatically. It is a slow achievement as we work day in and day out to locate ourselves within God's story. We inherently resist such a locating because we have come to love our sinfulness—and we fear losing it.

In this respect the emphasis in recent theology on sin as a fundamental orientation of self, rather than sin being associated with certain wrongful acts, is essentially correct. For example, O'Connell tries to provide this kind of interpretation of sin by utilizing the notion of "fundamental option."

> Mortal sin as an act is nothing else than a synonym for fundamental option. A mortal sin . . . is the act by which we substantially reject God and assume instead a posture apart from and in alienation from God. Mortal sin is the moment in which we deny the God who calls us through and in creation and thus, paradoxically, deny our deepest selves. Mortal sin is the act of sin by which we take upon ourselves the state of sin.
>
> But if mortal sin is nothing else than a negative fundamen-

tal option, it follows that, like that option, it is a transcendental act. That is, mortal sin is not precisely the doing of any particular categorical act. Rather it is the act of self-disposition occurring *through* and *in* that concrete categorical act.[21]

One can appreciate what O'Connell is trying to say. He rightly wants to emphasize that sin reaches and determines the fundamental orientation of the self, that is, it determines our very relationship with God. Yet he wants to avoid the idea that sin is a given, but then neither is it a matter of choice. What then is it? It seems he needs an account of the self in which our actions are rooted in what most nearly makes us what we are, so that sin becomes the qualification of the self rather than of actions. But the language of "fundamental option" does not really serve his purpose, since to protect self-freedom the "fundamental option" must be free of determination by our actions or history. He thus seems caught on the horns of a dilemma by locating sin in "transcendental freedom," for it is not clear how sin can reach to the depths of who we are and still be something we do.

But if there is no self more fundamental than our character, problems like this do not arise. Rather our sin consists in our allowing our character to be formed by the story that we must do everything (pride) or nothing (sloth).[22] There are so many different forms that pride and sloth take that we can use a bit of both of them in the complex stories that become ourselves. Indeed, as we look back on our lives our sin is more like something we discover than something we have done.

For our sin lies precisely in our unbelief—our distrust that we are creatures of a gracious creator known only to the extent we accept the invitation to become part of his kingdom. It is only by learning to make that story—that story of God—our own that we gain the freedom necessary to make our life our own. Only then can I learn to accept what has happened to me (which includes what I have done) without resentment. It is then that I am able to accept my body, my psychological conditioning, my implicit distrust of others and myself, as mine, as part of my story. And the acceptance of myself as a sinner is made possible only because it is an acceptance of God's acceptance. Thus I am able to see myself as a sinner and yet to go on.

This does not mean that tragedy is eliminated from our lives; rather we have the means to recognize and accept the tragic without turning to violence. For finally our freedom is learning how to exist in the world, a violent world, in peace with ourselves and others. The violence of the world is but the mirror of the violence of our lives. We say we desire peace, but we have not the souls for it. We fear the boredom peace seems to imply. Even more we fear the lack of control a commitment to peace would entail. As a result the more we seek to bring "under our control," the more violent we have to become to protect what we have. And the more violent we allow ourselves to become, the more vulnerable we are to challenges.

For what does "peace with ourselves" involve? It surely does not mean that we will live untroubled—though it may be true that no one can really harm a just person. Nor does it mean that we are free of self-conflict, for we remain troubled sinners—indeed, that may well be the best description of the redeemed. To be "at peace with ourselves" means we have the confidence, gained through participation in the adventure we call God's kingdom, to trust ourselves and others. Such confidence becomes the source of our character and our freedom as we are loosed from a debilitating preoccupation with ourselves. Moreover by learning to be at peace with ourselves, we find we can live at peace with one another. And this freedom, after all, is the only freedom worth having.

4. On Beginning in the Middle: Nature, Reason, and the Task of Theological Ethics

1. THE TASK OF CHRISTIAN ETHICS

It seems a little odd at this point to ask what the task of Christian ethics might be. Surely that should have been first on the agenda. In fact I have already started to do some Christian ethics insofar as I have argued that Christian ethics has a peculiar stake in narrative, vision, the virtues, and character as constituents of the moral life. For, as we saw, it is impossible to delineate the central concepts of an ethic without exposing the material content, the particular convictions, of that ethic. So in a sense one can ask about the task of Christian ethics only after it has begun.

But the matter is even more complex than this. For example, it seems straightforward enough to suggest that the primary task of Christian ethics is to understand the basis and nature of the Christian life. Yet a phrase like "understand the basis and nature of the Christian life" is filled with ambiguity. Does "understand" imply that the task is primarily descriptive? Is the chief concern to map the relation between Christian belief and behavior? Or does "understand" involve a normative task? Is the task of Christian ethics to recommend what we ought to do?

While I hope to show that Christian ethics is at once descriptive and normative, the interrelation between these tasks is complex and not easily stated. However, before such questions can even be investigated we need to remind ourselves that Christian ethics is not any distinct discipline but varies from time to time and from one to another ecclesial tradition. As we shall see, how Christian ethics is understood has always been dependent on its context in a specific tradition.

The development of moral theology in Roman Catholicism through the centuries became tied to the penitential system. Moral theologians aided confessional practice as they developed the casuistical detail necessary to sustain and inform the priestly function. Thus the study of moral theology was primarily a task performed by priests and through their preaching and confessional practice they helped the community determine minimum standards of behavior. Such an approach was not minimalistic in principle but became so precisely because the primary concern of the confessional was with avoiding evil.[1]

Although moral theologians served an ecclesial function, their work was thought to be based primarily on "natural law." This may well suggest that the alleged transparency of the natural law norms reflects more the consensus within the church than the universality of the natural law itself. I suspect that "natural law," rather than indicating agreement between Christian and non-Christian, served to note agreements within a widely scattered and pluralistic Christian community. This is substantiated by the fact that the power of natural law as a systematic idea was developed in and for the Roman imperium and then for "Christendom." Thus, ironically, "natural law" became the means of codifying a particular moral tradition.

Because of the very problems it was asked to address, this form of Christian ethics tended to be act-oriented. Though it was often systemized in the language of the virtues, it evidenced little concern for or analysis of the actual development of virtue but instead concentrated on the fulfillment of specified duties. Moral theologians came to look more like lawyers than theologians. They were people skilled in adjudication of cases for the troubled conscience (no mean or small skill).

Moreover, even though they were called "theologians," these moralists seldom were required to make direct theological appeals. Theological claims set the backdrop that made their work intelligible —e.g., God is the creator of a rational universe and moral law can be thus known without the aid of revelation. Beyond that, little theological reflection was required for explicating the nature of the Christian moral life. Thus "theology" in the phrase "moral theology" denoted an unquestioned ecclesial assumption rather than an enlivening practice.

In fairness it should be said that Catholicism included other ways of thinking about the moral life, for example, spiritual and ascetical theology. Yet these forms of literature were not considered "ethics" since they did not deal with specific judgments of right and wrong. Moreover, much of the ascetical literature was devotional in character and, thus, was not meant as a means to explore systematic issues.

In contrast, theological issues always have been at the forefront of Protestant ethical reflection. In fact Protestants did not develop any specialized discipline called "Christian ethics" until recently. Of course they did not have the confessional, as did Catholics, but that was not the decisive reason for their lack of any explicit discipline called Christian ethics. Rather the Protestant emphasis on God's free grace made "ethics" an inherently doubtful enterprise, since "ethics," from such a perspective, appeared as an attempt to presumptively determine God's will or to substitute works for faith. Indeed some could go as far as to suggest that ethics is sin insofar as it tries to anticipate God's will.[2]

This is not to say that there was no concern for ethics in the Protestant tradition; rather it was included as part of the theologians' task. Thus "ethics" involved discussion of the relation of law and gospel, creation and redemption, faith and works, the status of the orders of creation, and the nature of man as sinner and redeemed. While such problems are central to the ethical task, theological discussions of this sort often failed to deal with the kind of moral concerns and issues that constitute how men and women in fact live. Certainly individual theologians often provided compelling accounts of human existence, but they were more likely to be interested in the systematic relations between the theological concepts than in the practical force such concepts might have for directing lives. Interestingly enough, the more concrete form of analysis undertaken to guide behavior among Protestants tended to be done pastorally and, as a result, was often not informed by explicit theological convictions.

Therefore, even though Protestant ethical reflection seemed richer theologically than Catholicism's, it tended to be as culturally assimilationist as the natural law tradition. In the absence of any disciplined and practical form of ethical reflection, Protestants could only assume that "Christian ethics" was little different from the consensus of whatever culture they found themselves a part. This is most strikingly illustrated by Protestantism's inability to be more than national churches.

In fairness it ought to be said that Christian ethics appears in a more distinct light in Calvinist, Anabaptist, and Anglican traditions, due to their stress on sanctification. Each of these traditions assumes that God's activity on our behalf entails a particular way of life that can be spelled out in some detail. Yet although such an assumption often produced reflection on the moral life meant to inform Christian consciences, it rarely produced a disciplined study called "Christian ethics" in any way comparable to Catholic moral theology.

In fact the very idea of Christian ethics is a relatively new phenomenon. In America it seems to have been primarily an outgrowth of the Social Gospel movement. It occasioned courses in Protestant seminaries dealing with "Christian sociology." Soon internal criticism of some of the enthusiasm of the Social Gospel required such courses to take a more reflective and critical standpoint. Thus the work of H. R. Niebuhr represents the attempt to make Christian ethics a discipline whose task is to clarify the moral implications of Christian theological convictions.[3] Such work is seen to be primarily analytical and descriptive, but without explicit normative prescriptions.

This brief and inadequate attempt to characterize Christian ethics in Catholic and Protestant traditions is meant only to make us aware that the activity we call "Christian ethics" is anything but singular or clear. For example, it is very interesting that we have no "Christian ethics" in the early church. Nowhere in Scripture do we get a distinction between religious belief and behavior. The Sermon on the Mount is hardly Jesus' "ethic," but is part and parcel of his proclamation of the coming kingdom. Paul's "ethics" is not really concerned with the status of the law. Scripture creates a problem in that its integration of belief and behavior makes it difficult to describe a "biblical ethic," let alone to discover in what manner it is still relevant for our current reflection.[4]

Neither is there much evidence that any of the church fathers thought it necessary to do ethics as an explicit task. Their explicit ethical reflections were primarily occasioned by their pastoral concerns. Thus they seldom give systematic presentations of the Christian life but engage in a sort of ad hoc reflection, since their primary concern was to respond to the needs of a particular community. Indeed, there is something to be said for still labeling ethics a pastoral discipline.

Nor do we get "ethics" as separate treatises in the highly systematic Middle Ages. Aquinas never stopped to say: "Now I am going to do a little ethics." The "ethics" he does in the Prima-Secundae and Secunda-Secundae of the *Summa Theologica* is but the continuation of his theological portrayal of God's extension of himself to man so that man might have a way to God.[5] "Ethics" is not done as an independent discipline, but because such considerations are necessary to depict our journey with God.

So what are we to make of the fact that we now have a discipline called Christian ethics, that practitioners are armed with Ph.D.'s in the subject and are ready to apply their skills? Why should this be the case? Not every tradition feels the need to develop a distinct discipline called "ethics." Perhaps part of the reason for the concern with Christian ethics has to do with the cultural situation depicted in chapter 1. Because many of the "natural" relations that people used to assume between religious belief and behavior have been broken, we hope that if we think hard enough about those relations we can again reestablish their essential connection. Such a task is unfortunately doomed to failure. For finally these relations are not conceptual, but practical. Christian ethics, as a critical and reflective discipline, cannot restore what only a community can hold together. Christian ethics, insofar as it is an intelligible discipline at all, is dependent on a community's wisdom about how certain actions are prohibited or enjoined for the development of a particular kind of people.

That such is the case, however, helps us understand better the task of Christian ethics. For it makes clear that Christian ethics is not an abstract discipline primarily concerned with "ideas." Rather it is a form of reflection in service to a community, and it derives its character from the nature of that community's convictions. Theological claims are fundamentally practical and Christian ethics is but that form of theological reflection which attempts to explicate this inherently practical nature.

1.1   Christian Ethics Is Theology

As should be obvious from the above I have little interest in trying to claim that Christian ethics is a coherent subdiscipline within the wider discipline of theology. Indeed, I think in many ways the separation of ethics from theology has had unfortunate consequences. Ethics is but one aspect of the theological task and little hangs on whether it has integrity as a specifiable discipline.

Yet it is important not to be too humble about this. For at the same time it is crucial that Christian ethics not be understood as an afterthought to systematic theology. If theological convictions are meant to construe the world—that is, if they have the character of practical discourse—then ethics is involved at the beginning, not the end, of theology. Theological discourse is distorted when portrayed as a kind of primitive metaphysics—a view all too common among Protestants as well as Catholics. That is, Catholics often assume that one must start with fundamental theology, which investigates the conditions of truthfulness, the metaphysical presuppositions (natural theology) which make theology at all possible. Then one proceeds to systematic theology, which deals with revelational claims such as trinity, creation, redemption, Christology, church, and so on. Finally, when that work is done, one turns to ethics on the assumption that only when one's basic beliefs are clear and well-founded can one consider their moral implications. Ironically this picture usually results in a theological justification for basing ethics on a natural law methodology, with the result that theological convictions about Jesus are not directly relevant to concrete ethical analysis.

Even though Protestants have been less confident in natural theology or a natural law ethic, they also assume theology begins primarily with prolegomena. Also, especially since the nineteenth century, they have tried to prepare the way for doing theology with anthropology, attempting to show the intelligibility of theological claims. Often what was done in that respect was "ethical" insofar as ethics is understood to involve accounts of human existence, but this often resulted in theology being no more than, in Karl Barth's memorable phrase, "talking about man in a loud voice."

In contrast to both these approaches I wish to show that Christian ethics is not what one does after one gets clear on everything else, or after one has established a starting point or basis of theology; rather it is at the heart of the theological task. For theology is a practical activity concerned to display how Christian convictions construe the self and world.[6] Therefore theological claims concerning the relation of creation and redemption are already ethical claims, since they situate how one works methodologically. Put more strongly, ethics has been artificially separated from the central theological task exactly because of the abstract way in which the relation between creation and redemption, nature and grace, has been understood.

1.2   Nature and Grace: Why Being Christian Is Not Equivalent to Being Human

The abstractions "nature" and "grace" in particular have distorted how ethics has been undertaken in the Catholic tradition. This is true despite the fact that there is a concern afoot in the Catholic Church that moral theology be more explicitly theological. For example, the "Decree of Priestly Formation" of Vatican II explicitly charged: "Its [moral theology's] scientific exposition should be more thoroughly nourished by scriptural teaching. It should show the nobility of the Christian vocation of the faithful and their obligation to bring forth fruit in charity for the life of the world."[7] Yet the theological presuppositions on which the structure of Roman Catholic ethics is built assume that is exactly what cannot be done. Unfortunately, much of contemporary Catholic ethics, while often beginning with some theological rhetoric, continues to rest finally on an anthropological foundation. For example Timothy O'Connell says,

> . . . the fundamental ethical command imposed on the Christian is precisely to be what he or she is. "Be human." That is what God asks of us, no more and no less. Imitate Christ, and do this by seeking to be as faithful to the human vocation as he was. Love your neighbor as yourself. Do unto others as you would have them do unto you. Christian ethics is human ethics, no more and no less. . . . Christians are unconditionally humanists; that is our pride and our privileged vocation. . . . Thus in a certain sense, moral theology is not theology at all. It is moral philosophy, pursued by persons who are believers. Moral theology is a science that seeks to benefit from all the sources of wisdom within our world.[8]

Such a position is bound to use Christ to underwrite the integrity of the "natural," since he is seen as epitomizing the fulfillment of the human vocation. Again O'Connell says, "It is the faithful articulation of the meaning of Jesus' call that we should 'be what we are.' "[9] Apart from the fact that this seems to be very bad advice—as Mark Twain observed, the worst advice you can give anyone is to be himself—such an approach jeopardizes the attempt to make theological convictions more ethically relevant.

In fairness it should be noted that O'Connell has a chapter dealing with "elements" of a biblical morality. The covenant, kingdom, repentence, discipleship, law, and love each receive brief treatment and review. But these "elements" are not methodologically decisive for how O'Connell does ethics.[10] That such is the case, however, is not accidental, but structured into the way O'Connell understands what Christianity is about. Christian ethics is human ethics because the particularity of Jesus, his historicity as God's decisive eschatological actor, has been lost. Thus, according to O'Connell,

> What must not be debated is the fact that incarnation *could* have taken place apart from original sin. Inasmuch as this world was created as a potential receptacle for the divinity of God's Word, incarnation was possible from the first moment of creation. Therefore, even if the *function* of incarnation was (at least in part) the rectification of the evil situation of mankind, such was not the *essence* of the incarnation. No, the essence of incarnation was simply the self-gift of God to his people, the union

of God, through his Word, with the good world which had come from his creative hand.[11]

Apart from the dubious wisdom of talking about the *"essence of the incarnation,"* the problem with such Christology is that it results in making the events and actions of Jesus' life seem accidental. Incarnation is not an adequate summary of the story. Rather "incarnation" is but one of the conceptual reminders that the church has developed to help us tell well the story of the man who was nothing less than the God-appointed initiator of the new kingdom.

This kind of theological abstractionism is a characteristic of both Catholic and Protestant ethics. Theological concepts are reifications; they are taken as the "meat," the point, of Christian convictions. But as abstractions both "nature" and "grace" require more determinative narrative display.[12] There is no creation without the covenant with Israel, there is no redemption that does not take its meaning from Jesus' cross.[13] Neither are they general concepts that straightforwardly describe or gain their meaning from human existence per se; rather the concepts of both creation and redemption are aids to train us to be creatures of a gracious God who has called us to be citizens in a community of the redeemed.

When nature-grace, creation-redemption are taken to be the primary data of theological reflection, once they are abstracted from the narrative and given a life of their own, a corresponding distortion in moral psychology seems to follow. Since the material content—that is, the rightness or wrongness of certain behavior—is derived from nature, Christian convictions at best only furnish a motivation for "morality." As Joseph Fuchs says,

> The specific and *decisively Christian* aspect of Christian morality is not to be sought first of all in the particularity of categorical values, virtues, and norms of various human activities. Rather it resides in the believer's fundamental Christian decision to accept God's love in Christ and respond to it as one who believes and loves, as one who assumes the responsibility for life in this world in imitation of Christ, that is, as one who has died with Christ and is risen with him in faith and sacrament thus becoming a new creation.[14]

Fuchs calls this "Christian intentionality" the "deepest and most challenging element of morality, which addresses the whole person, and not only the individual deed."[15] Such intentionality "pervades" particular categorical conduct, but it does not determine its content. "This means that truthfulness, uprightness, and faithfulness are not specifically Christian, but generally human values in what they materially say, and that we have reservations about lying and adultery not because we are Christians, but simply because we are human."[16] Thus the meaning of the "Christianum" for our concrete living is to be found in its "motivating power."[17]

But to reduce the "Christianum" to the motivational distorts our moral psychology since it presupposes that virtues such as truthfulness can be "objectively" characterized abstracted from how agents must learn to be truthful. Therefore the very integrity of self, the character required for moral agency, is lost. For, as we saw in the preceding chapter, our very ability to be moral agents is dependent on our having a character that forges a link between what we do and what we are.

Likewise, when Christian convictions are relegated to the "motivational" part of our lives the historical dimension of the self is irretrievably lost. We have character just to the extent that we can claim our history as our own, but when our actions are separated from our history, when we are only the "causes" of certain pieces of behavior, we lose exactly what is necessary to be historic. There is, perhaps, a correlation between Christian ethicists' penchant for theological abstractions divorced from their narrative context and the tendency to develop a "natural law" ethic that is free from historic communities.

But it may be objected that surely I am too hard on this attempt to reinterpret natural law in terms of "humanity," for it is surely a step in the right direction. What possibly could be wrong with the claim that to be Christian is to be fully human? No one wants to maintain that there is an essential discontinuity between God's creating and redeeming work, between nature and grace. Surely what it means to be Christian is but an intensification, not a denial, of what it means to be human.

Of course that is correct, but at issue is the methodological significance it has for ethical reflection. To be Christian is surely to fulfill the most profound human desires, but we do not know what such fulfillment means on the basis of those desires themselves. It is certainly right that life in Christ makes us more nearly what we should be, but that is not to say we must start with the human to determine what it means to be a disciple of Christ. While the way of life taught by Christ is meant to be an ethic for all people, it does not follow that we can know what such an ethic involves "objectively" by looking at the human.

Moreover such a view optimistically assumes that in fact we know morally in what such a universal or objective ethic consists. As we saw above, Fuchs has an extraordinary confidence that we are, in fact, in possession of common moral intuitions and values such as truthfulness, uprightness, and faithfulness. But he does not provide a concrete analysis of those "values" sufficient to indicate why the understanding of "truthfulness" differs from society to society. I have no reason to deny that human nature may well require a fundamental orientation to truth, but I do not think it possible to abstract such truthfulness from its various narrative contexts in order to make it the basis of a "universal" and "objective" ethic.

1.3   Church and World: The Ethics of a Critical Community

The affirmation that Christian ethics is human ethics contains yet another dubious assumption, this time about the relation of church and world. Richard McCormick, a Catholic moralist like O'Connell and Fuchs, says:

> Love and loyalty to Jesus Christ, the perfect man, sensitizes us to the meaning of persons. The Christian tradition is anchored in faith in the meaning and decisive significance of God's covenant with men, especially as manifested in the saving incarnation of Jesus Christ, his eschatological kingdom which is here aborning but will finally only be given. Faith in these events, love of and loyalty to this central figure, yields a decisive way of viewing and intending the world, of interpreting its meaning, of hierarching its values. In this sense the Christian tradition only illumines human values, supports them, provides a context for their reading at given points in history.[18]

But McCormick does not tell us what, if anything, such an illumination adds to the ethical; in effect he assumes that the primary task of Christian convictions is to "support" human values. But this assumption presumes that Christians will never be radically anti-world —that is, aligned against the prevailing values of their cultures. In fact behind the emphasis on the "human" character of Christian ethics is a deep fear that there might be a radical discontinuity between Christians and their culture. The result, I fear, is that too often natural law assumptions function as an ideology for sustaining some Christians' presuppositions that their societies—particularly societies of Western democracies—are intrinsic to God's purposes.[19]

McCormick says, "If Christian faith adds new material (concrete, behavioral) content to morality, then public policy is even more complex than it seems. For example, if Christians precisely as Christians know something about abortion that others cannot know unless they believe it as Christians, then in a pluralistic society there will be problems with discussion and decision in the public forum."[20] But why does he assume that the public forum is shaped by "human" values? Why does he assume that Christians should be able to contribute to the "public forum" on its own terms? What, for example, would have been the result if Christians had approached their entry into Roman society with McCormick's presuppositions? Isn't it possible that Christians, because of the ethos peculiar to their community, might find themselves in deep discontinuity with the ethos of a particular society?

Therefore the question of the distinctiveness of Christian ethics—or as I have put it, the insistence on the significance of the qualifier—also involves questions of the relationship of church to world. Indeed, how the task of Christian ethics is to be conceived is as much an ecclesiological issue as an issue having to do with nature and grace, creation and redemption. In fact, the issues are closely interrelated, since often how church is understood in relation to world follows from how nature and grace are thought to be related.

Of the two, however, the issue of the relation of church and world is more primary.[21] By virtue of the distinctive narrative that forms their community, Christians are distinct from the world. They are required to be nothing less than a sanctified people of peace who can live the life of the forgiven.[22] Their sanctification is not meant to sustain the judgment that they are "better" than non-Christians, but rather that they are charged to be faithful to God's calling of them as foretaste of the kingdom. In this sense sanctification is a life of service and sacrifice that the world cannot account for on its own grounds.

Therefore, claims for the distinctiveness of the church, and thus Christian ethics, are not attempts to underwrite assumptions of superiority or Christian dominance. Rather they are meant to remind Christians of the radicalness of the gospel. For the gospel cannot be adequately summed up by appeals that we should love our neighbor as ourselves but is meant to transform us by teaching us to be God's peaceable people.

Emphasis on the distinctiveness of Christian ethics does not deny that there are points of contact between Christian ethics and other forms of the moral life. While such points frequently exist, they are not sufficient to provide a basis for a "universal" ethic grounded in human nature per se. Attempts to secure such an ethic inevitably result in a minimalistic ethic and often one which gives support to forms of cultural imperialism. Indeed, when Christians assume that their particular moral convictions are independent of narrative, that they are justified by some universal standpoint free from history, they are tempted to imagine that those who do not share such an ethic must be particularly perverse and should be coerced to do what we know on universal grounds they really should want to do.

I do not mean to imply that adherents of a "natural law" ethic are inherently more violent, but rather that violence and coercion become conceptually intelligible from a natural law standpoint. The universal presumptions of natural law make it more difficult to accept the very existence of those who do not agree with us; such differences in principle should not exist. For example, natural law is often expressed today in the language of universal rights—the right to be free, to worship, to speak, to choose one's vocation, etc. Such language, at least in principle, seems to embody the highest human ideals. But it also facilitates the assumption that since anyone who denies such rights is morally obtuse and should be "forced" to recognize the error of his ways. Indeed, we overlook too easily how the language of "rights," in spite of its potential for good, contains within its logic a powerful justification for violence. Our rights language "absolutizes the relative" in the name of a universal that is profoundly limited and limiting just to the extent that it tempts us to substitute some moral ideal for our faithfulness to God.

To reiterate a point, recent attempts to identify Christian ethics with a universal human ethic fail to recognize that all accounts of the moral life are narrative dependent. We must recognize that, in MacIntyre's words, "action itself has a basically historical character. It is because we all live out narratives in our lives and because we understand our own lives in terms of narratives that we live out that the form of narrative is appropriate for understanding the actions of others. Stories are lived before they are told—except in the case of fiction."[23] Moreover, we must recognize that we live out our lives in the light of certain conceptions of a possible shared future. As a result I am not a self born with no history. Rather the story of my life "is always embedded in the story of those communities from which I derive my identity. I am born with a past; and to try to cut myself off from that past, in the individualist mode, is to deform my present relationships. The possession of an historical identity and the possession of a social identity coincide."[24]

Christian ethics involves the extraordinary claim that by learning to be faithful to the way of life inaugurated by Jesus of Nazareth we have, in fact, become part of the shared history that God intends for his whole creation. But that such an eschatological view is inherent in our morality does not mean that we can assume that the "universal" inclusion of all people in God's kingdom is an accomplished fact. Rather it means that as Christians we have been given the means to recognize ourselves for what we are—historic beings who must begin our ethical reflection in the midst of history.

There is no point outside our history where we can secure a place to anchor our moral convictions. We must begin in the middle, that is, we must begin within a narrative. Christianity offers a narrative about God's relationship to creation that gives us the means to recognize we are God's creatures. Thus it is certainly true that the God we find in the story of Jesus is the same God we find in creation— namely, the God who wills us to share in his life. We have a saving God, and we are saved by being invited to share in the work of the kingdom through the history God has created in Israel and the work of Jesus. Such a history completes our nature as well as our particular history by placing us within an adventure which we claim is nothing less than God's purpose for all of creation.

This implies, moreover, that Christian ethics does not, methodologically, have a starting point. The dilemma of whether we must do Christian ethics out of a doctrine of God or of man is a false one. For Christian ethics begins in a community that carries the story of the God who wills us to participate in a kingdom established in and through Jesus of Nazareth. No matter where it begins theologically, if it tries to do more or less than remind us of the significance of that story it has lost its way. Theology has no essence, but rather is the imaginative endeavor to explicate the stories of God by showing how one claim illuminates another.

Where does this leave the issue of how best to understand the relation of creation and redemption, nature and grace? Do I mean to defend a Christian ethic that stresses redemption and grace as in essential discontinuity with creation and nature? Decidedly no! God has never been other than a saving God. That is as true of God as creator as it is of God as redeemer. By emphasizing the narrative character of our knowledge of God I mean to remind us that we do not know what it means to call God creator or redeemer apart from the story of his activity with Israel and Jesus. The language of creation and redemption, nature and grace, is a secondary theological language, that is sometimes mistaken for the story itself. "Creation" and "redemption" should be taken for what they are, namely ways of helping us tell and hear the story rightly.

Moreover, if creation and redemption are assumed to be intelligible in themselves—that is, apart from the story—the kind of "saving" that we find in the life and death of Jesus Christ is distorted. That God "saves" is not a pietistic claim about my status individually. Salvation is not fundamentally some fresh and compelling insight about my life—though such insight may be included. Rather, the God of Israel and Jesus offers us salvation insofar as we are invited to become citizens of the kingdom and thus to be participants in the history which God is creating. This does not mean that nature is only "saved" as it becomes historical, but reminds that both nature and history are abstractions. What is redeemed is this or that creature who combines aspects of nature and history.

1.4   Summary of the Argument

Thus far I have tried to argue that the "natural law" starting point for Christian ethics, even in the updated form of "Christian ethics as human ethics" has the following difficulties: (1) It creates a distorted moral psychology, since the description of act is thought to be determined by an observer without reference to the dispositions of the agent. This leads to concentration on judgments about action from an observer's standpoint that the "new Catholic moralists" at least claim they want to avoid. (2) It fails to provide an adequate account of how theological convictions are a morality, i.e., that they are meant not just to describe the world but to form the self and community. (3) It confuses the claim that Christian ethics is an ethic that we should and can commend to anyone with the claim that we can know the content of that ethic by looking at the human. (4) It fails to appreciate that there is no actual universal morality, but that in fact we live in a fragmented world of many moralities. (5) Because it seems to entail a strong continuity between church and world, natural law ethics fails to provide the critical perspective the church needs to recognize and deal with the challenges presented by our societies and the inherent violence of our world. (6) It ignores the narrative character of Christian convictions by forgetting that nature-grace, creation-redemption are secondary theological concepts only intelligible in relation to the story of the God of Abraham, Isaac, Jacob, and Jesus. (7) It tempts us to coerce those who disagree with

us, since its presumptions lead us to believe that we always occupy
the high ground in any dispute.

2. REASON AND REVELATION

Many would argue there is another more serious problem with
my defense of a qualified ethic against natural law approaches. To
emphasize the revelation within the Christian community seems to
be anti-rational. For example, Richard McCormick says "if Christian
faith and revelation add material content to what is knowable in principle by reason, then the churches conceivably could teach moral
positions and conclusions independently of the reasons and analyses
that recommend these conclusions. This could lend great support to
a highly juridical and obediential notion of Christian morality."[25] At
the very least his claim seems doubtful in light of the history of the
use of "natural law" by church authorities to support authoritarian
positions. Indeed, I would suggest that part of the difficulty with the
moral reasoning supporting some of the church's sexual ethics is that
by attempting to give them a "natural law" basis devoid of their theological basis they appear arbitrary and irrational — thus requiring authoritarian imposition.

Yet the question McCormick raises is an important one since it
rightly concerns the questions of the kind and place of authority in
Christian ethics and of the relation of that authority to reason. In his
Authority in Morals Gerard Hughes gives a careful account of how
these questions might be approached from a natural law perspective.

[The] most obvious court of appeal in moral theology is the
teaching of Christian moral tradition, as this finds expression
either in the Bible or in later documents of that tradition. In
harmony with this approach is the view that there is a specifically Christian ethic, which it is the task of moral theology to ex-
pound by reflection on the data of the specifically Christian
revelation. In so far as this revelation is taken to be authoritative
in ethics, it is taken to be in some sense an ultimate, which is
not open to further criticism from sources external to itself.
Against this view, I propose two basic types of difficulty. The
first is theological in character. I argue that the picture of God
which inevitably emerges from this kind of approach is one
which Christians are themselves unwilling to accept consistent-

ly. On this model, I argue God must emergy as an arbitrary
figure who would have no legitimate claim on our belief or our
allegiance; yet one of the clearest themes of the Judaeo-Chris-
tian tradition in the Bible is that God is someone whom man
can accept as the ultimate answer to his legitimate aspirations.
Any theory of revelation which denies this must in the end leave
revelation itself deprived of its credentials. In particular, God
must be seen as morally acceptable if we are to have any reason
for believing that it is indeed God who is speaking to us.
Secondly, I propose some more philosophical objections to this
position. It is characteristic of the Christian religion that God
reveals himself in history, and therefore in a particular culture
at a particular time and place. The texts of Christian tradition
in which that revelation is communicated to us are, by the same
token, texts of a particular human community at different peri-
ods of its development. As such, these texts raise all the philosophical problems of interpretation and translation raised by
any text. It follows that the meaning of these texts cannot simply be read off automatically from the texts themselves. In order
to establish their meaning we have to have recourse to other
assumptions and arguments which the texts themselves do not
provide.[26]

Interestingly, Hughes advances his argument with confidence
that he knows what "morality" involves. He says,

The distinctive, and objectionable, contention of the voluntarist
is that even given the creation of man, what is right and wrong
for men to do depends on a *further* act of God's will; God could
have placed us under different, incompatible, obligations while
leaving us unaltered. In thus severing the connection between
the nature of man and the moral obligations under which God
could place him, the voluntarist renders man's moral perfection
unintelligible, because it is no longer related to any other facet
of man's development. He therefore runs the risk of making his
God arbitrary. In the main, Christian tradition has rejected this
picture of God as inconsistent with his character that has been
revealed to us and with the ways in which his moral concern for
us has been shown.[27]

Now Hughes's argument against arbitrariness works only when
we assume we know the nature and content of morality prior to our
knowledge of God. Hence, it is odd that Hughes appeals to revela-

tion in order to deny that Christian ethics is based on revelation—
i.e., that revelation which "has been revealed to us and with the ways
in which his moral concern for us has been shown." Clearly Hughes
must have two different senses of revelation at work, and this is but
an indication that we need to know better what he means by "revelation." In one form he seems to identify revelation as a category of
knowledge that cannot be rationally justified—but that is surely a
mistake.

It is a mistake because first of all the word "revelation" is not a
qualifier of the epistemic status of a kind of knowledge, but rather
points to the content of a certain kind of knowledge. We call knowledge about God "revelation" not because of the rationality or irrationality of such knowledge, but because of what that knowledge is
about. It certainly is true that our knowledge of God may challenge
certain accounts of what counts as rational, but that does not mean
that revelation is thereby irrational. Revelation is properly a description of that knowledge that bears the stamp of God and God's saving
intentions, but that stamp is not thereby necessarily discerned in a
mysterious manner, though knowledge of revelation may well be
knowledge of a mystery. To say knowledge is "revealed" marks it as
being about God, in contrast to so much of our knowledge that
makes no attempt to tell us about God.

It has become popular to say that revelation is not concerned
with propositions, but is instead the self-disclosure of God. Thus
many speak of "revelatory events"—the "Exodus event" or the "resurrection event." They often wish to suggest that revelation does not
make claims about what happened, but about the meaning of what
happened. In contrast, it is my contention that revelation involves
propositional claims, none of which can be isolated by themselves,
but are intelligible only as they form a coherent narrative.

From this perspective I find the traditional distinction between
natural knowledge of God and revelation to be misleading. All
knowledge of God is at once natural and revelatory. But like all
knowledge it depends on analogical control. Analogies, in turn, derive their intelligibility from paradigms that draw on narratives for
their rational display.[28] Our narratives of God's dealing with us in-
spire and control our attempt to test how what we know of God helps
us understand why the world is as it is—i.e., finite.

But our knowledge of God is also moral. For example, our
avowal of God's perfection is that of a being with complete integrity.
Put simply, there is no underside to God's intentions. God is what
God does in a manner unlike anyone or anything else. God's good-

ness therefore is not like our goodness, for a perfect faithfulness is God's very nature. That God is moral in this sense is the basis for our confidence that we are more nearly ourselves when we are like God. Christian morality, therefore, cannot but require us to become faithful imitators of God.

This in fact is a familiar biblical concern. For example, consider the language of *Leviticus* 19:1-4:

> And the Lord said to Moses, "Say to all the congregation of the people of Israel, You shall be holy; for I the Lord your God am holy. Every one of you shall revere his mother and his father, and you shall keep my sabbaths: I am the Lord your God. Do not turn to idols or make for yourselves molten gods. I am the Lord your God."

Or again *Leviticus* 19:11-12:

> "You shall not steal, nor deal falsely, nor lie to one another. And you shall not swear by my name falsely, and so profane the name of your God: I am the Lord."

The biblical Commandments do not command us arbitrarily; rather they call us to be holy as God is holy, as we have learned of holiness through God's faithfulness to us. Therefore, like God we are called to be what we are and to do what we do (e.g., we leave part of our fields unharvested for the poor) because God is that kind of God. Such a morality requires no "foundation"; it is enough that we know it to reflect the very nature of God.

It may be objected that the sense of "holiness" in these verses is rather abstract, but such a charge can only be sustained by ignoring the narrative displays of God's holiness in Scripture: it is God who has brought us from the land of Egypt, who has given us the judges, prophets, and priests. As Christians we claim we learn most clearly who God is in the life and death of Jesus Christ. By learning to "imitate" Jesus we in fact become part of God's very life and therein find our true home. We become holy by becoming citizens in God's kingdom, thereby manifesting the unrelenting love of God's nature.

If we have a "foundation" it is the story of Christ. "For no other foundation can anyone lay than that which is laid, which is Jesus Christ" (1 Cor. 3:11). Here Paul speaks not of some form of individualistic perfection, but rather of the building of a community — a body of people. But such a people can survive only if their commitments to one another are built on commitment to Christ.

Such a foundation is not extra-rational; indeed, it is a claim about reality—namely, that our existence is God-given and -formed. Such a claim is properly interpreted, as are all claims, within a community that seeks to understand its world. At least the beginning of wisdom in human communities is the recognition that our lives are narrative dependent, that we are pilgrims on a journey, even if we are not sure what that journey entails. That we Christians witness to a man's life, a man called Jesus, who is the heartbeat of our life and the meaning and form of our existence becomes intelligible (and therefore rational) in the light of such narrative dependency.

It is our conviction that we are provided with a truthful account of reality that enables us to see our life as more than a succession of events when we learn to locate our story in God's story. That does not mean our life has a singular goal or meaning; rather, the story of God we learn through Christ gives us the skills to go on even when no clear goal is present. We rightly seek neither happiness nor pleasure in themselves; such entities are elusive. Rather we learn happiness and pleasure when we find in a faithful narrative an ongoing and worthy task that is able to sustain our lives.

By learning to understand ourselves as creatures, as beings open to the redemption made possible by Jesus' preaching of the kingdom, we are able to place ourselves within God's story. As creatures we learn to understand our lives as a story God is telling:

> a story which begins in the primeval creative utterance and which will one day, having reached its appointed conclusion, end. Only the Author of the drama is in a position to specify clearly the ultimate significance of the roles which particular creatures are called upon to play. Only he may finally see how the various roles make up a coherent whole. The creature who plays his role may be very uncertain whether the story is now in its final chapters or whether the plot is really just beginning to get off the ground. In short, the creature is not responsible for the whole of the story or for all the consequences of his action. Rather, he is responsible for playing well the role allowed him. To understand ourselves as creatures is to believe that we ought not step out of the story and think of ourselves as author rather than character. We are not to orchestrate the final denouement; we are simply to be responsible.[29]

Put simply, we Christians are not called on to be "moral" but faithful to the true story, the story that we are creatures under the Lordship of a God who wants nothing more than our faithful service. By such service we become not "moral," it seems, but like God, holy.

but only the Jesus given to us by the early church, which had its own particular axes to grind. There is no alternative but to provide a "hermeneutical principle" prior to the Gospels that can establish Jesus' nature and significance.

Yet there is a deep difficulty with the strategy that attempts to avoid dealing with Jesus as he is portrayed in the Gospels. Christologies which emphasize the cosmic and ontological Christ tend to make Jesus' life almost incidental to what is assumed to be a more profound theological point. In particular the eschatological aspects of Jesus' message are downplayed. Yet there is widespread agreement that one of the most significant "discoveries" of recent scholarship is that Jesus' teaching was not first of all focused on his own status but on the proclamation of the kingdom of God.[1] Jesus, it seems, did not direct attention to himself, but through his teaching, healings, and miracles tried to indicate the nature and immediacy of God's kingdom.[2] It may be objected that even this conclusion about him seems to presuppose exactly what we just said could *not* be assumed—namely, that we are able to isolate the real Jesus from the Jesus created by the early churches. Yet we can at least say that Jesus as depicted in Mark, Matthew, and Luke does not call attention to himself, but to the kingdom which the early Christians felt had been made present and yet was still to come.

It is not my intention to settle to what extent we can know the "real Jesus." I am quite content to assume that the Jesus we have in Scripture is the Jesus of the early church. Even more important, I want to maintain that it cannot or should not be otherwise, since the very demands Jesus placed on his followers means he cannot be known abstracted from the disciples' response. The historical fact that we only learn who Jesus is as he is reflected through the eyes of his followers, a fact that has driven many to despair because it seems they cannot know the real Jesus, in fact is a theological necessity. For the "real Jesus" did not come to leave us unchanged, but rather to transform us to be worthy members of the community of the new age.

It is a startling fact, so obvious that its significance is missed time and time again, that when the early Christians began to witness to the significance of Jesus for their lives they necessarily resorted to a telling of his life. Their "Christology" did not consist first in claims about Jesus' ontological status, though such claims were made; their Christology was not limited to assessing the significance of Jesus' death and resurrection, though certainly these were attributed great significance; rather their "Christology," if it can be called that,[3] showed the story of Jesus as absolutely essential for depicting the kind of kingdom they now thought possible through his life, death, and resurrection. Therefore, though Jesus did not call attention to himself, the early Christians rightly saw that what Jesus came to proclaim, the kingdom of God as a present and future reality, could be grasped only by recognizing how Jesus exemplified in his life the standards of that kingdom.

But the situation is even more complex. The form of the Gospels as stories of a life are meant not only to display that life, but to train us to situate our lives in relation to that life. For it was assumed by the churches that gave us the Gospels that we cannot know who Jesus is and what he stands for without learning to be his followers. Hence the ironic form of Mark, which begins by announcing to the reader this is the "good news about Jesus, the anointed one, the son of God," but in depicting the disciples shows how difficult it is to understand the significance of that news. You cannot know who Jesus is after the resurrection unless you have learned to follow Jesus during his life. His life and crucifixion are necessary to purge us, like his disciples and adversaries had to be purged, of false notions about what kind of kingdom Jesus has brought. Only by learning to follow him to Jerusalem, where he becomes subject to the powers of this world, do we learn what the kingdom entails, as well as what kind of messiah this Jesus is.

Like Mark, my own emphasis on the ethical significance of Jesus' life and the necessity of attending to the narrative portrait of that life, is different from that usually given in Christian ethics. Indeed that very way of putting it — i.e., the ethical significance of Jesus — is misleading. For it is not as though we can know Jesus or understand him apart from his ethical significance. To locate our lives in relation to his is already to be involved with the basic issues of Christian ethics. Jesus is he who comes to initiate and make present the kingdom of God through his healing of those possessed by demons, by calling disciples, telling parables, teaching the law, challenging the authorities of his day, and by being crucified at the hands of Roman and Jewish elites and raised from the grave. Insisting that Jesus is the initiator and presence of the kingdom, of course, does not mean he was not the Christ, or that he is not God incarnate, or that his death and resurrection has nothing to do with the forgiveness of sins, but it does mean that each of these claims are subsequent to the whole life of this man whom God has claimed as decisive to his own for the presence of his kingdom in this world.

Indeed it is interesting to note that when the fathers wish to explicate the word "incarnation" in speaking of Jesus, the word they use is "economy," which simply means how God manages the world. So for Athanasius the incarnation notes how God's economy—that is, God's Word—appropriated a human body so that he might die and be raised.[4] Thus incarnation is not a doctrine that places all significance on the birth of Jesus, nor is it a doctrine about Jesus' person or nature, but it is a reminder that we cannot assess God's claim of Jesus' significance short of seeing how his whole life manifests God's kingdom.[5]

My emphasis on Jesus' life as depicted by the early church is not, therefore, an example of a "low Christology." Indeed it is my contention that by attending to the narrative form of the Gospels we will see all the more clearly what it means for Jesus to be God's anointed. By learning to be followers of Jesus we learn to locate our lives within God's life, within the journey that comprises his kingdom. I will try to show how the very heart of following the way of God's kingdom involves nothing less than learning to be like God. We learn to be like God by following the teachings of Jesus and thus learning to be his disciples.

For we have been told:

> "You have heard that it was said, 'An eye for an eye and a tooth for a tooth.' But I say to you, Do not resist one who is evil. But if any one strikes you on the right cheek, turn to him the other also; and if any one would sue you and take your coat, let him have your cloak as well; and if any one forces you to go one mile, go with him two miles. Give to him who begs from you, and do not refuse him who would borrow from you.
>
> "You have heard that it was said, 'You shall love your neighbor and hate your enemy.' But I say to you, 'Love your enemies and pray for those who persecute you, so that you may be sons of your father who is in heaven; for he makes his sun rise on the evil and on the good, and sends rain on the just and the unjust. For if you love those who love you what reward have you? Do not even the tax collectors do the same? And if you salute only your brethren, what more are you doing than others? Do not even the Gentiles do the same? You, therefore, must be perfect, as your heavenly Father is perfect.' " (Matt. 5:38–48)

We are called to be like God: perfect as God is perfect. It is a perfection that comes by learning to follow and be like this man whom God has sent to be our forerunner in the kingdom. That is why Christian ethics is not first of all an ethics of principles, laws, or values, but an ethic that demands we attend to the life of a particular individual—Jesus of Nazareth. It is only from him that we can learn perfection—which is at the very least nothing less than forgiving our enemies.

2. JESUS, ISRAEL, AND THE IMITATION OF GOD

The theme of "imitation" is subject, however, to much misunderstanding. In particular, it carries with it individualist presuppositions that are antithetical to the social nature of the Christian life. For there is no way to learn to "imitate" God by trying to copy in an external manner the actions of Jesus. No one can become virtuous merely by doing what virtuous people do. We can only be virtuous by doing what virtuous people do in the manner that they do it. Therefore one can only learn how to be virtuous, to be like Jesus, by learning from others how that is done. To be like Jesus requires that I become part of a community that practices virtues, not that I copy his life point by point.

There is a deeper reason that I cannot and should not mimic Jesus. We are not called upon to be the initiators of the kingdom, we are not called upon to be God's anointed. We are called upon to be *like* Jesus, not to *be* Jesus. As I will try to show, that likeness is of a very specific nature. It involves seeing in his cross the summary of his whole life. Thus to be like Jesus is to join him in the journey through which we are trained to be a people capable of claiming citizenship in God's kingdom of nonviolent love—a love that would overcome the powers of this world, not through coercion and force, but through the power of this one man's death.

A proper appreciation of the centrality of the theme of imitation must begin, however, not with Jesus but with Israel. For Jesus brought no new insights into the law or God's nature that Israel had not already known and revealed. The command to be perfect as God is perfect is not some new command, nor is the content of that command to love our enemies new. Both the structure and the content of the command draw from the long habits of thought developed in Israel through her experience with the Lord. Jesus' activity as presented in the Gospels makes no sense without assuming what Israel had long known, that any story worth telling about the way things are requires an account of God's activity as the necessary framework for that story.

It was Israel's conviction, as displayed in the Hebrew Scriptures, that a series of events in her history was decisive for God's relation to mankind. In these events God had spoken, and Israel constantly returned to them to guide her future relations with God. For the interpretation that came to be put on the journey of Moses from Egypt was such that the Exodus, "the law-giving at Sinai, the crossing of Jordan, the temple on Zion were seen as the formative phases in God's creation of his people Israel. . . . The life of the people of God had necessarily to retain (through 'remembering' and 'meditation') an intimate organic relation to this vital formative period of their history, because in it the essential shape of life had been clearly indicated by God himself. In this sequence of history God had shown that he is always *prevenient*: life is a journey where he goes before men as guide and as example; and that he is always *provident*: he accompanies them as their companion and instructor, and, as it turns out in the end, he is himself the route."[6]

Therefore the task for Israel, indeed the very thing that makes Israel Israel, is to walk in the way of the Lord, that is, to imitate God through the means of the prophet (Torah), the king (Sonship), and the priest (Knowledge).[7] To walk in the way of God meant that Israel must be obedient to the commands (Deut. 8:6); to fear the Lord (Deut. 10:12); to love the Lord (Deut. 11:22); and thus to be perfect in the way (Gen. 17:1). But the way of obedience is also the way of intimacy, for Israel is nothing less than God's "first-born son" (Ex. 4:22). Moreover Israel has the knowledge of the Lord as a just and compassionate God and so Israel too must act justly and with compassion. (Jer. 22:16).

Israel is Israel, therefore, just to the extent that she "remembers" the "way of the Lord," for by that remembering she in fact imitates God. Such a remembering was no simple mental recollection, rather the image remembered formed the soul and determined future direction. "To remember the works of Yahweh and to seek him, i.e., to let one's acts be determined by his will, is in reality the same. Consequently, to 'remember' the 'Way' from the Reed Sea onwards is to act *now* on the basis of the relationship between God and Israel there revealed, and in so doing to appropriate it, and know it to be most real."[8] Thus the call of the prophets to Israel was always a summons to return to the vocation of an *imitator Dei*: God "asks of men that they shall reflect his own character, so far as it can be reflected within the limitations of human life. . . . When the prophets denounced harshness and oppression and called for compassion for the unfortunate, they were calling men to reflect the character which was uniquely expressed in God's deliverance of his people."[9] For Israel, therefore, to love God meant to learn to love as God loved and loves.

> The Lord set his heart upon your fathers and chose their descendants after them, you above all peoples, as at this day. . . . For Yahweh your God is God of gods and Lord of lords, the great, the mighty, and the terrible God, who is partial and takes no bribe. He executes justice for the fatherless and the widow, and loves the sojourner, giving him food and clothing. Love the sojourner therefore; for you were sojourners in the land of Egypt. You shall fear the Lord your God; you shall serve him and cleave to him, and by his name you shall swear. . . . You shall therefore love the Lord your God, and keep his charge, his statutes, his ordinances, and his commandments always. (Deut. 10:15ff.)

Each of the major offices in Israel — king, priest, and prophet — also drew its substance from the need for Israel to have a visible exemplar to show how to follow the Lord.[10] What was needed were people who embodied in their lives and work the vocation of Israel to "walk" in the "way" of the Lord. The king, the prophet, and the priest were judged by how well they dedicated their lives to being suitable models for the people to imitate. As a result there was a clear tendency in Israel for the three functions to coalesce in one figure — for example, Moses or the servant in the "Servant" songs of Isaiah. For, like the prophet, the servant is predestined (Isa. 49:1) and called by God for a special task. But the servant is also commissioned to be a king, to walk in the way of the Torah of the Lord. Even more, the servant becomes the priestly sacrifice, giving himself for the people. By enacting in his life these offices, the servant displays to Israel not only their task, but the very life of God.

It is against this background that the early Christians came to understand and believe in Jesus' life, death, and resurrection. They had found a continuation of Israel's vocation to imitate God and thus in a decisive way to depict God's kingdom for the world. Jesus' life was seen as the recapitulation of the life of Israel and thus presented the very life of God in the world. By learning to imitate Jesus, to follow in his way, the early Christians believed they were learning to imitate God, who would have them be heirs of the kingdom.

How Jesus' life was seen as the recapitulation of God's way with Israel is perhaps nowhere better presented than in the temptation narratives. For in the wilderness Jesus, like Israel, discovers his vocation through being tempted to pervert God's gifts to Israel. In the first temptation we see Jesus so identified with Israel that he experiences Israel's perennial desire for certainty of her own choosing. Is he to be like Moses and turn stone to bread? Surely it would be a good thing to turn stone to bread, to be a ready resource to feed the hungry and the poor. But Jesus rejects that means of proving how God reigns with his people knowing that the life offered Israel is more than bread can supply. (Luke 4:4).

Again the devil tempts him, this time with dominion, with kingship even greater than that of the great David. It is a dominion that can bring peace to the nations, since one powerful king can force all to his will. But again Jesus rejects such dominion. God's kingdom, it seems, will not have peace through coercion. Peace will come only through the worship of the one God who chooses to rule the world through the power of love, which the world can only perceive as weakness. Jesus thus decisively rejects Israel's temptation to an idolatry that necessarily results in violence between peoples and nations. For our violence is correlative to the falseness of the objects we worship, and the more false they are, the greater our stake in maintaining loyalty to them and protecting them through coercion. Only the one true God can take the risk of ruling by relying entirely on the power of humility and love.

Finally, Jesus is tempted to act as the priest of priests, to force God's hand by being the sacrifice that God cannot refuse. In short, Jesus is tempted to play the hero, to take his life in his hands, to be in control of his destiny, and thus to force God's kingdom to be present because of his sacrifice. But such a heroic role contrasts starkly with the man who died on the cross, subject to others' wills. For by being so subject we see that finally it is not his will but God's that is worked out through his life and death. The resurrection, therefore, is not an extra-ordinary event added to this man's life, but a confirmation by God that the character of Jesus' life prior to the resurrection is perfectly faithful to his vocation to proclaim and make present God's kingdom. Without the resurrection our concentration on Jesus would be idolatry, but without Jesus' life we would not know what kind of God it is who has raised him from the dead.

The temptation narratives are but a particularly concentrated example of how the early church understood Jesus' life as recapitulating the life of the Lord with Israel. The baptism, the turning to Jerusalem, the cleansing of the temple, the last supper, the crucifixion, and the resurrection were equally understood to be the deliberate representing of Jesus as Israel's king-messiah. But also the calling of the twelve, the necessity of wandering throughout Israel, the signs on the sabbath, the desert feedings, and the special attention to the poor and the outcast are understood to be at once recapitulation and innovation of the life of Israel and her relationship to God.[11] Thus it is not surprising that the early Christians assumed that by imitating the "Way" of Jesus they were imitating the "Way" of God himself. For the content of the kingdom, the means of citizenship, turns out to be nothing more or less than learning to imitate Jesus' life through taking on the task of being his disciple.

And one becomes a disciple by following the way of God, which is the way of renunciation: "If any man would come after me let him deny himself and take up his cross and follow me" (Mark 8:34). Moreover, such a renunciation is not merely an existential giving up of the self, but the surrender of family life and affection (Matt. 10:37), and perhaps even the giving up of life itself (Mark 10:45).[12] But it is also a life of humility:

> You know that those who are supposed to rule over the Gentiles lord it over them and their great men exercise authority over them. But it shall not be so among you; but whoever would be great among you must be your servant, and whoever would be first among you must be slave of all. For the Son of man also came not to be served but to serve, and to give his life as a ransom for many. (Mark 10:42–45)

In this way of service we learn of the kind of God we are to love and to whom we are called to obedience. For Jesus' life is the life of God insofar as he serves others as God serves us.

> His first allegiance is to God; then he loves the neighbor as himself. So he has no need to lord over out of fear or to get others to serve him; and his commitment to serve is courageous, for he loses his life by so doing. So Jesus' idea of service does not become a matter of doing what others want him to do except insofar as it remains consonant with his understanding of God's will. He will heal others who request it, like Bartimaeus, but he will not grant the request of James and John who want power and glory. Strong-willed and independent, Jesus has a clear sense of his own mission, and neither traditions nor laws nor public pressure nor fear of indictment prevent him from speaking or acting.[13]

Thus Jesus' whole life, as narratively depicted in the Gospels, is a life of power that is possible only for one possessed by the power of God. But such a power, exactly because it is a genuine and truthful power, does not serve by forcing itself on others. Thus he "calls" the disciples and teaches them to be faithful, but he does not try to control their responses. He knows that the form of power which results from our being dispossessed of the powers currently holding our lives can come only as we freely give up those things and goods that possess us. But we do not dispossess ourselves just by our willing, but by being offered a way of selfless power. Thus Jesus finally goes to his death not knowing what the future behavior of the disciples might be or their ultimate fate. He dies out of obedience and entrusts the future to God.

In like manner Jesus serves those he would help and those he must confront. In response to people's faith he heals, crediting not his own authority but the person's faith and God's power as the source of healing. He does not seek out those to heal, for he came out to preach, but he heals those who come to him. Moreover, he serves the authorities by confronting them. "Jesus confronts the authorities with the nature of God's rule and with the seriousness of their offenses against it, but he does not impose his authority on them. After each confrontation, he moves on, leaving the authorities to choose their response. He is not a military messiah who uses a sword or manipulates the crowds to impose his authority. He does not even fight to defend himself, and he endures the consequences of his opponent's scorn."[14]

In Jesus' life we cannot help but see God's way with Israel and Israel's subsequent understanding of what it means to be God's beloved. For God does not impose his will upon her. Rather he calls her time and time again to his way, to be faithful to the covenant, but always gives Israel the possibility of disobedience. It is thus in the cross that Christians see the climax of God's way with the world. In his cross we see decisively the one who, being all-powerful, becomes vulnerable even to being a victim of our refusal to accept his Lordship. Through that cross God renews his covenant with Israel; only now the covenant is with the "many." All are called to be his disciples through this one man's life, death and resurrection, for in this cross we find the very passion of God. We are therefore invited to drink this drink, and to be baptized with this baptism (Mark 10:39), and in doing so we believe that we become participants in God's very life. In short, we begin to know what it means to imitate God.

3. JESUS AND THE KINGDOM OF GOD

But we must remember that for Israel to imitate God or for Christians to imitate Jesus is not an end in itself. Such an imitation is to put one in the position of being part of a kingdom. As we have already noted, Jesus as portrayed in the synoptic Gospels does not call attention to himself. He comes to announce the kingdom as a present reality. To what extent he understood then how his life would be chosen by God to be the means by which that kingdom would be made a reality to all people, we have no way of knowing. What is significant is not what Jesus may or may not have thought about himself, though he certainly acted as one having authority (Matt. 12:28), but that he was obedient to his calling and therefore is the sign and form of the reality of God's kingship then and now.

To begin to understand Jesus' announcement of the kingdom we must first rid ourselves of the notion that the world we experience will exist indefinitely.[15] We must learn to see the world as Israel had learned to understand it — that is, eschatologically. Though it sounds powerful and intimidating, in fact it is quite simple, for to view the world eschatologically is to see it in terms of a story, with a beginning, a continuing drama, and an end. And "a story needs an ending. A point must be reached at which one can feel that certain issues are resolved, a certain finality has been achieved. In this respect a story departs from real life. In reality there never is an end. . . . But the story-teller cannot accept this. . . . The story-teller needs finality, a closed sequence of events such that a judgment can be passed."[16] It is against this background that Jesus' announcement of the kingdom must be seen, for he came to announce an end that, while not yet final, nonetheless provided a necessary perspective for our continuing life in the world.

It has long been noted that in the Gospels we have texts that indicate variously that the kingdom is coming, that it is present, and that it is still to come. Several theories have been proposed as to how these statements might be reconciled. Some suggest that one or another tense cannot have been Jesus' own words. They either identify him with the more immediate apocalyptic expectation or suggest that he saw the kingdom to come in the future. I would agree, however, with A. E. Harvey that the whole question is irresolvable in the terms in which it is raised.[17] Not only do we lack the means to know what is Jesus' view and that of the early church, but it by no means follows that Jesus had a rigorously consistent view. Moreover by letting the issue be dominated by the question of "when?" we miss the more important question of the "what?"

The kingdom is not simply some cipher that we can fill in with our ideas about what a good society ought to look like. Nor is it merely a way of reemphasizing the eternal sovereignty of God, though this is certainly part of what the proclamation of the kingdom entails. Rather the proclamation of the coming kingdom of God, its presence, and its future coming is a claim about *how* God rules and the establishment of that rule through the life, death, and resurrection of Jesus. Thus the Gospels portray Jesus not only offering the possibility of achieving what were heretofore thought to be impossible ethical ideals. He actually proclaims and embodies a way of life that God has made possible here and now.

Jesus directs our attention to the kingdom, but the early followers rightly recognized that to see what that kingdom entailed they must attend to his life, death, and resurrection, for his life reveals to us how God would be sovereign. Therefore to learn to see the world eschatologically requires that we learn to see the life of Jesus as decisive for the world's status as part of God's kingdom.

Just as we cannot understand what it means to learn to follow Jesus without understanding what it means for Israel to be on a journey with the Lord, so we cannot understand the kingdom without understanding its role in Israel. The kingdom ideal that Jesus proclaimed is no new idea nor does he seem to have given it some startling new meaning. Rather he proclaims that the kingdom is *present* insofar as his life reveals the effective power of God to create a transformed people capable of living peaceably in a violent world.

Israel as God's chosen, as I have already suggested, had been schooled to look on the world eschatologically. That she could do so depended on her knowing who it was that gave her the destiny to be the people of God. That is, she knew who her true king was — the Lord of Abraham, Isaac, and Jacob. It was this Lord who established the covenant with her, who gave her the law, who gave her the land, who fought to secure the land. It was this Lord who appointed a king, who sent the prophets, and who provided the means to worship and holiness. Thus what made Israel Israel was her steadfast devotion to the true Master of the universe.

Yet there were in Israel differences about what acknowledgment of God's sovereignty entailed — differences that were still being debated and acted on during Jesus' lifetime. For some, to worship God as king meant the refusal to call any man master, even if that man was Caesar. Thus some, in the name of Yahweh's sovereignty, thought such allegiance entailed the obligation to try to free Israel, if necessary by violent means, from her masters. Judas the Galilean revolted against Rome and a Roman census on the grounds that submitting to Roman rule amounted to a denial of the Lord. Drawing on the holy war tradition, he believed that God is the God of battles, who will help his people overthrow and destroy their enemies.[18]

An alternative understanding of God's sovereignty was that created by piety. In this view, to affirm God as King does not entail violent overthrow of those who currently hold the power of the state, but the creation of a sphere of life through the law where God's will dominates.

> Thus the affirmation of God's sole kingship implies not military revolt but the submission of one's whole life to the regulations of the Torah, notably to its ritual prescriptions. It means severing oneself from all that is outside the realm of God's rule, viz., from all who do not 'take the yoke upon themselves'. . . . Taking the yoke of the kingdom upon oneself is associated with the necessity of daily set prayers and of following a complex set of ritual prescriptions. We may reasonably conjecture that the God who is addressed as King in such prayers is conceived of as a God of holiness and purity such that he will not tolerate the presence of that which is ungodly, impure, polluted.[19]

There were many variations of these alternatives alive in Israel prior to and during Jesus' life. Some, rejecting both alternatives, tended in a more apocalyptic direction. "If the time was short and judgment strictly by the Law, then the appropriate course was to withdraw as far as possible from the contamination of the world and prepare oneself by asceticism, study and discipline."[20] Thus the sects rejected both the gradualism of the Pharisees and the self-initiated violence of the revolutionaries.

No doubt Jesus' and the early church's understanding of the kingdom bore similarities to each of these alternatives. It seems likely, however, that Jesus' understanding was most similar to that represented by the Pharisees.

> Like them, he offered a way of life in which religion would seem relevant to every activity; like them, he based his teaching on the will of God as revealed in the law; like them, he addressed much of his teaching to a public far wider than his immediate followers. But at the same time the differences are striking. On three matters which were of central importance to the Pharisees —a detailed code of observances, a careful selectiveness in the company they kept, and a concern for the authority of the tradition in which they stood—Jesus adopted a radically different stance.[21]

made possible by the resurrection. Through this crucified but resurrected savior we see that God offers to all the possibility of living in peace by the power of forgiveness.

It is crucial that we understand that such a peaceableness is possible only if we are also a forgiven people. We must remember that our first task is not to forgive, but to learn to be the forgiven. Too often to be ready to forgive is a way of exerting control over another. We fear accepting forgiveness from another because such a gift makes us powerless — and we fear the loss of control involved. Yet we continue to pray, "Forgive our debts." Only by learning to accept God's forgiveness as we see it in the life and death of Jesus can we acquire the power that comes from learning to give up that control. Freed from our need to coerce, we learn

> "not to be anxious about your life, what you shall eat or what you shall drink, nor about your body, what you shall put on. Is not life more than food, and the body more than clothing? Look at the birds of the air: they neither sow nor reap nor gather into barns, and yet your heavenly Father feeds them. Are you not of more value than they? And which of you by being anxious can add one cubit to his span of life?" (Matt. 6:25–27)

It is true, of course, that in a sense to be a "forgiven people" makes us lose control. To be forgiven means that I must face the fact that my life actually lies in the hands of others. I must learn to trust them as I have learned to trust God. Thus it is not accidental that Jesus teaches us to pray for our daily bread. We cannot live to insure our ultimate security, but must learn to live on a day-to-day basis. Or, perhaps better, we must be a people who have learned not to fear surprises as a necessary means to sustain our lives. For, ironically, when we try to exclude surprise from our life, we are only more subject to the demonic. We become subject to those "necessities" that we are anxious about because without them we fear we lack the power to control our lives.

But because we have learned to live as a forgiven people, as a people no longer in control, we also find we can become a whole people. Indeed the demand that we be holy is possible only because we find that we can rest within ourselves. When we exist as a forgiven people we are able to be at peace with our histories, so that now God's life determines our whole way of being — our character. We no longer need to deny our past, or tell ourselves false stories, as now we can accept what we have been without the knowledge of our sin destroying us.

Here we see the essential links between learning to live as a forgiven people, accepting our historicity, and being at peace with ourselves and with one another, for we are able to have a past only to the extent that we are able to accept forgiveness for what we have done and have not done but which we must claim as our own if we are to have a worthy history.[25] My sin is inexorably part of me, but I now no longer need to deny it. As I learn to locate my life within the kingdom of forgiveness found in Jesus' life, death, and resurrection, I acquire those virtues of humility and courage that are necessary to make my life my own.

That we are only able to have a history, a self, through the forgiveness wrought by God means that the resurrection of Jesus is the absolute center of history. It is on the basis of the resurrection that we can have the confidence to remember the history of our sin. Through the resurrection, by being invited to recognize our victim as our hope, we are gifted with the power to break the hold of our most determined oppressor—ourselves. As Rowan Williams has suggested, "the Christian proclamation of the resurrection of the crucified just man, his return to his unfaithful friends and his empowering of them to forgive in his name offers a narrative structure in which we can locate our recovery of identity and human possibility, a paradigm of the 'saving' process; yet not only a paradigm. It is a story which is itself an indispensable agent in the completion of this process, because it witnesses to the one personal agent in whose presence we may have full courage to 'own' ourselves as sinners and full hope for a humanity whose identity is grounded in a recognition and affirmation by nothing less than God. It is a story which makes possible the comprehensive act of *trust* without which growth is impossible."[26]

Only if our Lord is a risen Lord, therefore, can we have the confidence and the power to be a community of forgiveness. For on the basis of the resurrection we have the presumption to believe that God has made us agents in the history of the kingdom. The resurrection is not a symbol or myth through which we can interpret our individual and collective dyings and risings. Rather the resurrection of Jesus is the ultimate sign that our salvation comes only when we cease trying to interpret Jesus' story in the light of our history, and instead we interpret ourselves in the light of his.[27] For this is no dead Lord we follow but the living God, who having dwelt among us as an individual, is now eternally present to us making possible our living as forgiven agents of God's new creation.

Because we Christians believe we worship a resurrected Lord, we can take the risk of love. Thus we are told in 1 John 4:13–21:

By this we know that we abide in him and he in us, because he has given us of his own spirit. And we have seen and testify that the Father has sent his son as the Savior of the world. Whoever confesses that Jesus is the Son of God, God abides in him, and he in God. So we know and believe the love God has for us. God is love, and he who abides in love abides in God, and God abides in him. In this is love perfected with us, that we may have confidence for the day of judgment, because as he is so are we in this world. There is no fear in love, but perfect love casts out fear. For fear has to do with punishment, and he who fears is not perfected in love. We love, because he first loved us. If any one says, 'I love God,' and hates his brother, he is a liar; for he who does not love the brother whom he has seen, cannot love God whom he has not seen. And this commandment we have from him, that he who loves God should love his brother also.

This love that is characteristic of God's kingdom is possible only for a forgiven people — a people who have learned not to fear one another. For love is the nonviolent apprehension of the other as other. But to see the other as other is frightening, because to the extent others are other they challenge my way of being. Only when my self — my character — has been formed by God's love, do I know I have no reason to fear the other.

The kingdom of peace initiated by Jesus is also the kingdom of love which is most clearly embodied in the Christian obligation to be hospitable. We are community on principle standing ready to share our meal with the stranger. Moreover we must be a people who have hospitable selves — we must be ready to be stretched by what we know not. Friendship becomes our way of life as we learn to rejoice in the presence of others. Thus Jesus' kingdom is one that requires commitment to friends, for without them the journey that is the kingdom is impossible. We can only know where we walk as we walk with others.

5. AN ETHICS OF SALVATION AND FAITH

It may well be asked, "what has happened to the traditional Christian affirmations of salvation and faith in all this talk of the kingdom?" Has not the talk of peace and the necessity of our becoming peaceful members of God's kingdom come perilously close to turning the gospel into a moral ideal rather than the good news of salvation? For example, what are we to make of such a classical text as Romans 3:21-26:

> But now the righteousness of God has been manifested apart from law, although the law and the prophets bear witness to it, the righteousness of God through faith in Jesus Christ for all who believe. For there is no distinction; since all have sinned and fall short of the glory of God, they are justified by his grace as a gift, through the redemption which is in Christ Jesus, whom God put forward as an expiation by his blood, to be received by faith. This was to show God's righteousness, because in his divine forbearance he has passed over former sins; it was to prove at the present time that he himself is righteous and that he justified him who has faith in Jesus.

This Pauline emphasis on justification has sometimes been interpreted in a manner that amounts to a denial of the ethical. What is important is not that we are good or bad, that we do the right or wrong thing, but that we have faith. Of course, that does not mean that Paul is recommending that we sin, or that what Christians are and do have no relation to their "faith," but it is not at all clear from such a perspective how the "indicatives" of the faith — God has done X and Y for you — provide the rationale or justify the imperatives: Do this X or Y. To put it concretely, there seems to be a problem about how the admonitions Paul delivers in Romans 12 follow from and/or are integral to the claim of justification in Romans 3.

> Let your love be genuine; hate what is evil, hold fast to what is good; love one another with brotherly affection; outdo one another in showing honor. Never flag in zeal, be aglow with the Spirit, serve the Lord. Rejoice in your hope, be patient in tribulation, be constant in prayer. Contribute to the needs of the saints, practice hospitality. Bless those who persecute you; bless and do not curse them. Rejoice with those who rejoice, weep with those who weep. Live in harmony with one another; do not be haughty, but associate with the lowly, never be conceited. Repay no one evil for evil, but take thought for what is noble in the sight of all. If possible, so far as it depends upon you, live peaceably with all. Beloved, never avenge yourselves, but leave it to the wrath of God; for it is written, "Vengeance is mine, I will repay, says the Lord."

What does our having "faith" have to do with this way of life? Quite simply faith is our appropriate response to salvation, and it is fundamentally a moral response and transformation. Faith for Paul is not some mystical transformation of the individual; rather it is to be initiated into a kingdom. Faith is not belief in certain propositions, though it involves the attitude and passion of trust. Faith is not so much a combination of belief and trust, as simply fidelity to Jesus, the initiator of God's kingdom of peace.

> Therefore, since we are justified by faith, we have peace with God through our Lord Jesus Christ. Through him we have obtained access to this grace in which we stand, and we rejoice in our hope of sharing the glory of God. More than that, we rejoice in our sufferings, knowing that suffering produces endurance, and endurance produces character, and character produces hope, and hope does not disappoint us, because God's love has been poured into our hearts through the Holy Spirit which has been given to us (Rom. 5:1–5).

Faith is, in effect, finding our true life within the life of Christ. Thus in baptism we are literally initiated into his life.

> For if we have been united with him in death like his, we shall certainly be united in a resurrection like his. We know that our old self was crucified with him so that the sinful body might be destroyed, and we might no longer be enslaved to sin. For he who has died is freed from sin. But if we have died with Christ, we believe that we shall also live with him. For we know that Christ being raised from the dead will never die again; death no longer has dominion over him. The death he died he died to sin, once for all, but the life he lives he lives to God. So you also must consider yourselves dead to sin and alive to God in Christ Jesus. (Rom. 6:5–11)

But notice that this life is fundamentally a social life. We are "in Christ" insofar as we are part of that community pledged to be faithful to this life as the initiator of the kingdom of peace.

It is not that we have a prior definition of peace and then think of Christ as the great exemplar of that peace. Rather what Jesus has done enables us to know and embody God's peace in our lives by finding peace with God, with ourselves, and with one another. We have been justified because, as always, we find that our God has gone before, preparing the way for us to follow. But justification is only another way of talking about sanctification, since it requires our transformation by initiation into the new community made possible by Jesus' death and resurrection.

Of course, it may be objected that all this language about being a new people—a sanctified people—is a bit overblown. After all, Christians often times do not look very new; nor do we feel very new. We may claim that we are among the redeemed, but basically we feel pretty much the way we always do. The very idea that we are a holy people therefore seems overdrawn. Moreover, such language has the inevitable result of tempting us to self-righteousness. Perhaps it is better to face up to the fact that we are not the holy people, only more of the moderately good.

But this kind of thinking merely indicates that we have failed to let the challenge of the kingdom form our lives. For the language of "sanctification" and "justification" is not meant to be descriptive of a status. Indeed, part of the problem with those terms is that they are abstractions. When they are separated from Jesus' life and death, they distort Christian life. "Sanctification" is but a way of reminding us of the kind of journey we must undertake if we are to make the story of Jesus our story. "Justification" is but a reminder of the character of that story—namely, what God has done for us by providing us with a path to follow.

That I can and should grow into that story is not a claim about my moral purity, but denotes a wholeness of self that depends upon how far I have gone along that journey. My wholeness, my integrity, is made possible by the turthfulness of the story. Through the story of Jesus I can increasingly learn to be what I have become, a participant in God's community of peace and justice. Only by growing into that story do I learn how much violence I have stored in my soul, a violence which is not about to vanish overnight, but which I must continually work to recognize and lay down.

To do that I need skills—that is, I need to learn how to make my own the peace that comes from the knowledge that I am a creature of a gracious God. Such skills are not the sanctification of discrete actions, but the sanctification of the self as nonviolent. Sanctification is the formation of our lives in truth, since only such lives have the capacity for peace. Violence results from our attempting to live our lives without recognizing our falsehoods. Violence derives from the self-deceptive story that we are in control—that we are our own creators—and that only we can bestow meaning on our lives, since there is no one else to do so.

We mightily fear giving up our illusions; they are as dear to us as our selves. We fear if we learn to make the story of God our story we may have no self, no individuality left. Or that we will lose our autonomy. But the blessing lies in the irony that the more we learn to make the story of Jesus our story, the more unique, the more individual, we become — thus, the example of the saints.

Substantive stories cannot easily be made one's own. They challenge some of our most cherished illusions — for example, the illusion that we really want to know the truth about ourselves. True stories thus require extensive training in skills commensurate with that story. The Christian claim that life is a pilgrimage is a way of indicating the necessary and never-ending growth of the self in learning to live into the story of Christ. He is our master and from him we learn the skills to live faithful to the fact that this is God's world and we are God's creatures.

Though it is often tried, such skills can never be reduced to techniques. For example, learning to live in such a way that I need not fear death means coming to a real understanding that Jesus has for all times defeated death. The skill does not come easily, yet it is the truth. The challenge is in making it true for myself. But the good news is I cannot learn it by myself. We learn such a truth only by being initiated into it by others. That is why the question of the nature and form of the church is the center of any attempt to develop Christian ethics. And it is to that subject we must now turn.

6. The Servant Community: Christian Social Ethics

1. SOCIAL ETHICS AND QUALIFIED ETHICS

That this chapter is titled "Social Ethics" does not mean that what we have been doing up to this point has been something other than social ethics. Indeed the very claim that every ethic requires a qualifier involves social ethical assumptions, for it means that every ethic reflects a particular people's history and experience. For example, Christian ethics would be unintelligible if it did not presuppose the existence and recognizability of communities and corresponding institutions capable of carrying the story of God.

The most general name we give that community is church, but there are other names for it in the history of Christianity. It is "the way," the body of Christ, people of God, and a plethora of images that denote the social reality of being Christian and what it means to be a distinctive people formed by the narrative of God. We should remember that the name "church" is no less an image than "people of God." In fact, one of the issues in theology is which images of the church are primary or controlling for the others.

Thus, the claim that there is no ethic without a qualifier itself implies that a Christian ethic is always a social ethic. Indeed the notion that one can distinguish between personal and social ethics distorts the nature of Christian convictions, for Christians refuse to admit that "personal" morality is less a community concern than questions of justice, etc. "Personal" issues may, of course, present different kinds of concern to the community than does justice, but they are no less social for being personal.

At a general level there is much to be said for the contention that every ethic is a social ethic. The self is fundamentally a social self. We are not individuals who come into contact with others and then decide our various levels of social involvement. We are not "I's" who decide to identify with certain "we's"; we are first of all "we's" who discover our "I's" through learning to recognize the others as similar and different from ourselves. Our individuality is possible only because we are first of all social beings. After all, the "self" names not a thing, but a relation. I know who I am only in relation to others, and, indeed, who I am is a relation with others.[1]

But the claim that Christian ethics is a social ethic is even stronger than those now commonplace observations about the self's sociality. We have seen that the content of Christian ethics involves claims about a kingdom. Therefore the first words about the Christian life are about a life together, not about the individual. This kingdom sets the standard for the life of the church, but the life of the kingdom is broader than even that of the church. For the church does not possess Christ; his presence is not confined to the church. Rather it is in the church that we learn to recognize Christ's presence outside the church.

The church is not the kingdom but the foretaste of the kingdom. For it is in the church that the narrative of God is lived in a way that makes the kingdom visible. The church must be the clear manifestation of a people who have learned to be at peace with themselves, one another, the stranger, and of course, most of all, God. There can be no sanctification of individuals without a sanctified people. We need examples and masters, and if we are without either, the church cannot exist as a people who are pledged to be different from the world.

Therefore we see that contained in the claim that there is no ethic without a qualifier — a claim that at the beginning seemed to be primarily a methodological one — is a strong substantive assumption about the status and necessity of the church as the locus for Christian ethical reflection. It is from the church that Christian ethics draws its ethical substance and it is to the church that Christian ethical reflection is first addressed. Christian ethics is not written for everyone, but for those people who have been formed by the God of Abraham, Isaac, Jacob, and Jesus. Therefore Christian ethics can never be a minimalistic ethic for everyone, but must presuppose a sanctified people wanting to live more faithful to God's story.

The fact that Christian ethics begins and ends with a story requires a corresponding community existing across time. The story of God as told through the experience of Israel and the church cannot be abstracted from those communities engaged in the telling and the hearing. As a story it cannot exist without a historic people, for it requires telling and remembering if it is to exist at all. God has entrusted his presence to a historic and contingent community which can never rest on its past success, but must be renewed generation after generation. That is why the story is not merely told but embodied in a people's habits that form and are formed in worship, governance, and morality.

Therefore the existence of Israel and the church are not accidentally related to the story but are necessary for our knowledge of God. You cannot tell the story of God without including within it the story of Israel and the church. So it is not so odd that as part of the creed we affirm that we believe in the One Holy Catholic and Apostolic Church. We believe in the church in the sense that we know that it is not finally our creation, but exists only by God's calling of people. Moreover it is only through such a people that the world can know that our God is one who wills nothing else than our good. To be sure the church is often unfaithful, but God refuses to let that unfaithfulness be the last word. God creates and sustains a peaceable people in the world, generation after generation.

In a sense, the place of the Bible can be misleading in this respect, because it may appear that Scripture conveys the story regardless of the existence of a historic people. You do not need an intergenerational community. All you need is the story told rightly in a book. But the Bible without the community, without expounders, and interpreters, and hearers is a dead book.

Of course Scripture stands over the community exerting a critical function, but that it does so is an aspect of the community's self-understanding. Scripture is the means the church uses to constantly test its memory. That is why it can never be content with using just one part of Scripture, but must struggle day in and day out with the full text. For the story the church must tell as well as embody is a many-sided tale which constantly calls us from complacency and conventions. Scripture has authority in the church, not because no one knows the truth, but because the truth is a conversation for which Scripture sets the agenda and boundaries.[2] Those with authority are those who would serve by helping the church better hear and correspond to the stories of God as we find them in Scripture. Thus we are told

A dispute also arose among them, which of them was to be regarded as the greatest. And he said to them, 'The kings of the Gentiles exercise lordship over them; and those in authority over them are called benefactors. But not so with you; rather let the greatest among you become as the youngest, and the leader as one who serves. For which is the greater, one who sits at table,

or one who serves? Is it not the one who sits at the table? But
I am among you as one who serves.' (Luke 22:24–27)

2. THE CHURCH IS A SOCIAL ETHIC

But what does all this have to do with social ethics? This chapter
is supposed to be about Christians' social responsibility in the world,
but it does not seem we have been addressing that. What does this
emphasis on the church tell us about what we should be doing in
third-world countries? Or what we ought to be doing in this country
to ensure social justice? What should the Christian stance be about
the women's liberation movement? What should be our response to
war? These are the kinds of questions that are most often thought to
comprise social ethics, not questions about the place of Scripture in
the church's life.

Moreover once such questions are made central for determining
an agenda for a social ethic we feel the pull of natural law as an essential feature of Christian ethics. For to accomplish justice, to work for
a more nearly free and equitable social order requires cooperation
with non-Christians. If Christian social ethics depends on some
sources unique to being Christian, then it seems that our hope of
achieving more nearly just societies will be weakened; or even worse,
it seems to imply that Christians will seek to form Christian states or
societies (and we already know such societies whose histories of re-
pression and coercion make embarrassing reading). But surely in
matters of social ethics there must be moral generalities anchored in
our social nature that provide the basis for common moral commitment and action. Surely in social ethics we should downplay the
distinctively Christian and emphasize that we are all people of good
will as we seek to work for a more peaceable and just world for
everyone.

Yet that is exactly what I am suggesting we should not do. I am
in fact challenging the very idea that Christian social ethics is primarily an attempt to make the world more peaceable or just. Put starkly,
the first social ethical task of the church is to be the church — the servant community. Such a claim may well sound self-serving until we
remember that what makes the church the church is its faithful
manifestation of the peaceable kingdom in the world. As such the
church does not have a social ethic; the church is a social ethic.

The church is where the stories of Israel and Jesus are told, enacted, and heard, and it is our conviction that as a Christian people there is literally nothing more important we can do. But the telling of that story requires that we be a particular kind of people if we and the world are to hear the story truthfully. That means that the church must never cease from being a community of peace and truth in a world of mendacity and fear. The church does not let the world set its agenda about what constitutes a "social ethic," but a church of peace and justice must set its own agenda. It does this first by having the patience amid the injustice and violence of this world to care for the widow, the poor, and the orphan. Such care, from the world's perspective, may seem to contribute little to the cause of justice, yet it is our conviction that unless we take the time for such care neither we nor the world can know what justice looks like.

By being that kind of community we see that the church helps the world understand what it means to be the world. For the world has no way of knowing it is world without the church pointing to the reality of God's kingdom. How could the world ever recognize the arbitrariness of the divisions between people if it did not have a contrasting model in the unity of the church? Only against the church's universality can the world have the means to recognize the irrationality of the divisions resulting in violence and war, as one arbitrary unit of people seek to protect themselves against the knowledge of their arbitrariness.

The scandal of the disunity of the church is even more painful when we recognize this social task. For we who have been called to be the foretaste of the peaceable kingdom cannot, it seems, maintain unity among ourselves. As a result we abandon the world to its own devices. And the divisions I speak of in the church are not just those based on doctrine, history, or practices important though they are. No, the deep and most painful divisions afflicting the church are those based on class, race, and nationality that we have sinfully accepted as written into the nature of things.

Therefore the first social task of the church — the people capable of remembering and telling the story of God we find in Jesus — is to be the church and thus help the world understand itself as world. That world, to be sure, is God's world, God's good creation, which is all the more distorted by sin because it still is bounded by God's goodness. For the church to be the church, therefore, is not anti-world, but rather an attempt to show what the world is meant to be as God's good creation.

We must remember the "world" as that opposed to God is not an ontological designation. Thus "world" is not inherently sinful;

rather its sinful character is by its own free will. The only difference between church and world is the difference between agents. As Yoder suggests, the distinction between church and world is not between realms of reality, between orders of creation and redemption, between nature and supernature, but "rather between the basic personal postures of men, some of whom confess and others of whom do not confess that Jesus is Lord. The distinction between church and the world is not something that God has imposed upon the world by a prior metaphysical definition, nor is it only something which timid or pharisaical Christians have built up around themselves. It is all of that in creation that has taken the freedom not yet to believe."[3]

In this respect, moreover, it is particularly important to remember that the world consists of those, including ourselves, who have chosen not to make the story of God their story. The world in us refuses to affirm that this is God's world and that, as loving Lord, God's care for creation is greater than our illusion of control. The world is those aspects of our individual and social lives where we live untruthfully by continuing to rely on violence to bring order.

Church and world are thus relational concepts—neither is intelligible without the other. They are companions on a journey that makes it impossible for one to survive without the other, though each constantly seeks to do so. They are thus more often enemies than friends, an enmity tragically arising from the church's attempt to deny its calling and service to the world—dismissing the world as irredeemable, or transforming its own servant status into a triumphalist subordination of the world. But God has in fact redeemed the world, even if the world refuses to acknowledge its redemption. The church can never abandon the world to the hopelessness deriving from its rejection of God, but must be a people with a hope sufficiently fervid to sustain the world as well as itself.

That is why as Christians we may not only find that people who are not Christians manifest God's peace better than we ourselves, but we must demand that they exist. It is to be hoped that such people may provide the conditions for our ability to cooperate with others for securing justice in the world. Such cooperation, however, is not based on "natural law" legitimation of a generally shared "natural morality." Rather it is a testimony to the fact that God's kingdom is wide indeed. As the church we have no right to determine the boundaries of God's kingdom, for it is our happy task to acknowledge God's power to make his kingdom present in the most surprising places and ways.

Thus the church serves the world by giving the world the means to see itself truthfully. The social ethic of the church is, first of all, an affair of understanding rather than doing. The first question we must ask is not "what should we do," but "what is going on?"[4] Our interpretation will determine what we are to do. Our task as church is the demanding one of trying to understand rightly the world as world, to face realistically what the world is with its madness and irrationality.

Therefore calling for the church to be the church is not a formula for a withdrawal ethic; nor is it a self-righteous attempt to flee from the world's problems; rather it is a call for the church to be a community which tries to develop the resources to stand within the world witnessing to the peaceable kingdom and thus rightly understanding the world. The gospel is a political gospel. Christians are engaged in politics, but it is a politics of the kingdom that reveals the insufficiency of all politics based on coercion and falsehood and finds the true source of power in servanthood rather than dominion.

This is not to imply that the church is any less a human community than other forms of association. Just as in other institutions, the church draws on and requires patterns of authority that derive from human needs for status, belonging, and direction. The question is not whether the church is a natural institution, as it surely is, but how it shapes that "nature" in accordance with its fundamental convictions.[5] "Nature" provides the context for community but does not determine its character.

The church therefore is a polity like any other, but it is also *unlike* any other insofar as it is formed by a people who have no reason to fear the truth. They are able to exist in the world without resorting to coercion to maintain their presence. That they are such depends to a large extent on their willingness to move — they must be "a moveable feast." For it is certain that much of the world is bound to hate them for calling attention to what the world is. They cannot and should not wish to provoke the world's violence, but if it comes they must resist even if that resistance means the necessity of leaving one place for another. For as Christians we are at home in no nation. Our true home is the church itself, where we find those who, like us, have been formed by a savior who was necessarily always on the move.

3. A COMMUNITY OF VIRTUES

For the church to *be* rather than to *have* a social ethic moreover means that a certain kind of people are required to sustain it as an institution across time. They must, above all, be a people of virtue—not simply any virtue, but the virtues necessary for remembering and telling the story of a crucified savior. They must be capable of being peaceable among themselves and with the world, so that the world sees what it means to hope for God's kingdom. Such a people do not believe that everyone is free to do whatever they will, but that we are each called upon to develop our particular gifts to serve the community of faith.

That the church is God's creation does not mean it is any less human. The church bears the marks of natural communities, yet it does so as a graced community. James Gustafson has rightly argued that all human communities require virtues in order to be sustained. People in a community must learn to trust one another as well as trust the community itself.[6] Moreover, all communities require a sense of hope in the future and they witness to the necessity of love for sustaining relationships. Therefore there is a profound sense in which the traditional "theological virtues" of faith, hope, and love are "natural." As much as any institution the church is sustained by these "natural virtues."

But that does not mean that what is meant by faith, hope, and love is the same for Christians as for other people. For Christians, the sense of what it is in which they have faith, in which they hope, and the kind of love that must be displayed among them derives from the tradition that molds their community. Indeed, because of the character of that story, the nature and the meaning of the virtues are essentially changed. For Christians are the community of a new age which must continue to exist in the old age. Because of their existence between the times, because they are a people "on a way," they require, or perhaps better, make central, certain virtues that other communities do not.

Patience, for example, is one of the most needed virtues if we are to live amid this violent world as a peaceable people. Though we have learned to look on the present and future as God's kingdom and know that the kingdom has come in Jesus and is present in the breaking of bread, it is still to come. Sustained by its having come and fueled by its presence, we hope all the more in its complete fulfillment, but such a hope must be schooled by a patience. Otherwise our hope too easily turns to fanaticism or cynicism.

The church must learn time and time again that its task is not to *make* the world the kingdom, but to be faithful to the kingdom by showing to the world what it means to be a community of peace. Thus we are required to be patient and never lose hope. But hope in what? Specifically, hope in the God who has promised that faithfulness to the kingdom will be of use in God's care for the world. Thus our hope is not in this world, or in humankind's goodness, or in some sense that everything always works out for the best, but in God and God's faithful caring for the world.

Nowhere is the necessity of the interrelation of hope and patience better seen than in questions of justice. For it is a matter of justice that those who are hungry should be fed, that those who are abandoned should be cared for, that those who have been oppressed and maltreated should be freed and respected. Yet we know that while justice demands all these things, we live in a world where injustice seems to dominate. The hungry are fed, the abandoned cared for, the oppressed freed, it seems, only if there are enough resources that justice may be done without anyone else feeling the pinch.

When confronted with that reality a people who have been trained to hunger and thirst for righteousness, especially if they are no longer poor, can easily turn to violence. For how can we continue to face the poor without feeling the need to resort to coercion to see that even minimal justice be done? Moreover there is no question that violence works in some circumstances to relieve the burden of the poor. Indeed, one of their primary weapons is violence, since they are a people with nothing to lose—and such people are the most threatening of all for those of us who have something to lose. Most of us would rather bargain some of our possessions than have to deal with the threat of violence from those less fortunate.

But the justice that the church seeks is not derived from envy or fear. Rather we seek a justice that comes from a self-confident people who know their possessions are a gift in the first place. Therefore Christians cannot seek justice from the barrel of a gun; and we must be suspicious of that justice that relies on manipulation of our less than worthy motives, for God does not rule creation through coercion, but through a cross. As Christians, therefore, we seek not so much to be effective as to be faithful—we, thus, cannot do that which promises "results" when the means are unjust. Christians have rightly felt much in accord with those, such as Kant, who argue that there are some things we cannot do, no matter what good might accrue.

We must be a people who have learned to be patient in the face of injustice. But it may be objected: Surely that is too easily said if you are not the ones who are suffering from injustice. Precisely, but that does not mean that we ought to legitimize the use of force to overcome injustice. Such legitimation often comes from the attempt to have justice without risking the self, as when we ask the "state" or the "revolution" to see that justice is done, but in a manner that does not significantly affect our own material position. If we are to be a hopeful and patient people in a world of injustice, however, we cannot just identify with the "cause" of the poor, we must be like them poor and powerless.

Too often ideals and strategies for "social justice" are but formulas that attempt to make the poor and oppressed better off without requiring anything of us. But when we read that the poor, the merciful, peacemakers, the meek, the persecuted, the pure in heart are blessed, we can only presume those descriptions apply to anyone who would be a follower of Jesus. The question we must address to ourselves as Christians is: How is it that we who are Christians are so rich? And even more, how has our being such led us to misread the gospel as essentially an apolitical account of individual salvation, rather than the good news of the creation of a new community of peace and justice formed by a hope that God's kingdom has and will prevail.

Moreover the virtues of patience and hope are necessary to be a people who must learn to live without control. "Living out of control" has several senses, of course, not all of which are relevant for determining the character of the Christian community. For "living out of control" is but a way of suggesting that we are an eschatological people who base our lives on the knowledge that God has redeemed his creation through the work of Jesus of Nazareth. We thus live out of control in the sense that we must assume God will use our faithfulness to make his kingdom a reality in the world.

To live out of control, however, does not mean that we do not plan and/or seek to find the means to promote justice in the world, but that such planning is not done under the illusion of omnipotence. We can take the risk of planning that does not make effectiveness our primary goal, but faithfulness to God's kingdom. To plan in such a manner involves breaking the self-deception that justice can only be achieved through a power and violence that seeks to assure its efficacy.

For the irony is that no one is more controlled than those who assume they are in control or desire to be in control. It is the rich above all whose wealth gives them the illusion of independence, separateness, of "being in control." But all of us in one way or another willingly submit to the illusion that we can rid our world of chance and surprise. Yet when we do that our world becomes diminished as we try to live securely rather than well. For example, one of the things that happens to people in power is that they become controlled by their subordinates, who tell them only what they want to hear. They thus have no capacity to deal with the unexpected except by ignoring it, suppressing it, or eliminating it. They do not yet understand that the trick to living well is learning to make the unexpected our greatest resource.

Thus to live out of control means that we do not assume that our task as Christians is to make history come out right.[7] We do not need to write social ethics from the perspective of those who would claim to be in control and "in power." Rather we must assume that those who can more nearly give us a sense of what is really going on in the world are those who are "out of control." For those who are without control have fewer illusions about what makes this world secure or safe; and they inherently distrust those who say they are going to help through power and violence. Christian social ethics, therefore, is not best written from the perspective of the Secretary of State or the President, but from those who are subject to such people.

The task of the Christian people is not to seek to control history, but to be faithful to the mode of life of the peaceable kingdom. Such a people can never lose hope in the reality of that kingdom, but they must surely also learn to be patient. For they must often endure injustice that might appear to be quickly eliminated through violence. Moreover they can never acquiesce in the injustice, for to do so would only leave the neighbor to his or her own devices. Those who are violent, who are also our neighbors, must be resisted, but resisted on our terms, because not to resist is to abandon them to sin and injustice.

Such resistance may appear to the world as foolish and ineffective for it may involve something so small as refusing to pay a telephone tax to support a war, but that does not mean that it is not resistance. Such resistance at least makes clear that Christian social witness can never take place in a manner that excludes the possibility of miracles, of surprises, of the unexpected. As Yoder frankly states, "Christian ethics calls for behavior which is impossible except by the miracle of the Holy Spirit."[8] But that is the way it must be for a people who believe their very existence is nothing less than a continuing miracle.

4. THE "MARKS" OF THE CHURCH

For miracles happen here and there — indeed we believe the very existence of the church to be a miracle. However, to speak of the church as a continuing miracle simply does not sound like any church we know or experience. The church is not just a "community" but an institution that has budgets, buildings, parking lots, potluck dinners, heated debates about who should be the next pastor, and so on. What do these matters pertaining to the institutional form of the church have to do with the church as the miracle of God's continuing presence in our midst?

The people of God are no less an empirical reality than the crucifixion of Christ. The church is as real as his cross. There is no ideal church, no invisible church, no mystically existing universal church more real than the concrete church with parking lots and potluck dinners. No, it is the church of parking lots and potluck dinners that comprises the sanctified ones formed by and forming the continuing story of Jesus Christ in the world. In effect the church is the extended argument over time about the significance of that story and how best to understand it. There are certainly differences in the church which may even cause separation, but that is why the church should learn to value her heretics. We never know what it is we should believe or be until we are reminded by another.

No conversation over differences is more important than that between Israel and the church. For it is from Israel that we learn of the God who is present to us in the life, cross, and resurrection of Jesus. It is from Israel's continuing willingness to wait for the Messiah that we learn better how we must wait between the times. The church and Israel are two people walking in the path provided by God; they cannot walk independently of one another, for if they do they both risk becoming lost.[9]

The church, therefore, is not some ideal of community but a particular people who, like Israel, must find the way to sustain its existence generation after generation. Indeed, there are clear "marks" through which we know that the church is church. These marks do not guarantee the existence of the church, but are the means that God has given us to help us along the way. Thus the church is known where the sacraments are celebrated, the word is preached, and upright lives are encouraged and lived. Certainly some churches emphasize one of these "marks" more than others, but that does not mean that they are deficient in some decisive manner. What is important is not that each particular body of Christians does all of these things, but that these "marks" are exhibited by Christians everywhere.

The sacraments enact the story of Jesus and, thus, form a community in his image. We could not be the church without them. For the story of Jesus is not simply one that is told; it must be enacted. The sacraments are means crucial to shaping and preparing us to tell and hear that story. Thus baptism is that rite of initiation necessary for us to become part of Jesus' death and resurrection. Through baptism we do not simply learn the story, but we become part of that story. The eucharist is the eschatological meal of God's continuing presence that makes possible a peaceable people. At that meal we become part of Christ's kingdom, as we know there that death could not contain him. His presence, his peace is a living reality in the world. As his people we become part of his sacrifice, God's sacrifice, so that the world might be saved from sin and death.

These rites, baptism and eucharist, are not just "religious things" that Christian people do. They are the essential rituals of our politics. Through them we learn who we are. Instead of being motives or causes for effective social work on the part of Christian people, these liturgies *are* our effective social work. For if the church *is* rather than has a social ethic, these actions are our most important social witness. It is in baptism and eucharist that we see most clearly the marks of God's kingdom in the world. They set our standard, as we try to bring every aspect of our lives under their sway.[10]

Baptism and eucharist are our most fervent prayers and set the standard for all of our other prayers. For prayer is not our pleading to an unmoveable or unsympathetic, but all-powerful God. Rather it is through prayer that we learn to make ourselves open to God's presence. As Enda McDonagh has pointed out, prayer is the way we let God loose in the world.[11] Prayer, therefore, though a common activity, is a dangerous one, for God's presence is not easily controlled. God is a wild presence calling us to ways of life we had not imagined possible. Through baptism and the eucharist the Christian people open themselves to that wildness. It is no wonder that if possible the rulers would prevent Christians from praying, since there is no more powerful challenge to their power.

But Christians not only pray, they also preach. As we have seen there is no story without witness, and it is through the preaching of God's good news and our willingness to hear it that we become a people of witness. Preaching is not just the telling; it is also the hearing. Just as great art creates an audience capable of hearing or seeing in new ways, so the church's preaching creates an audience capable of being challenged by the story of Jesus and his kingdom. Our preaching, however, cannot be confined to ourselves, because we become witnesses to those who do not share our story. In fact, the very content of that story requires us to address the stranger. God has promised us that where the word is rightly preached (and heard), it will be fruitful. Through the witnessing to the story of Jesus Christ generation after generation, God will create a people capable of carrying into the world the story of Jesus and his kingdom.

Therefore, just as baptism and the eucharist are essential to the church's social ethic, so is our preaching. Our obligation to witness is an indication that for the Christian people there are no people beyond the power of God's word. Christians know no "barbarians," but only strangers whom we hope to make our friends. We extend hospitality to God's kingdom by inviting the stranger to share our story. Of course we know that the stranger does not come to us as a cipher, but the stranger also has a story to tell us. Through the stranger's reception of the story of Jesus (which may often take the form of rejection), we too learn more fully to hear the story of God. Without the constant challenge of the stranger—who often, interestingly enough, is but one side of ourselves—we are tempted to lose the power of Jesus' story because we have so conventionalized it.

But neither the marks of sacraments or preaching would be sufficient if the church was not also called to be a holy people—that is, a people who are capable of maintaining the life of charity, hospitality, and justice. Therefore the church cannot avoid the importance of mutual upbuilding and correction. We seek out the other because it is from the other that we learn how well or how poorly we have made the story of Jesus our story. For the church is finally known by the character of the people who constitute it, and if we lack that character, the world rightly draws the conclusion that the God we worship is in fact a false God.

It would be a mistake, moreover, to separate this emphasis on being a holy people from that of being a sacramental people. For I think it is not accidental that one of the classical eucharistic texts appears in the context of moral exhortation. In 1 Corinthians 11:17–26 Paul says,

> but in the following instructions I do not commend you, because when you come together it is not for the better but for the worse. For in the first place, when you assemble as a church, I hear that there are divisions among you; and I partly believe it, for there must be factions among you in order that those who are genuine among you may be recognized. When you meet together, it is not the Lord's supper that you eat. For in eating, each one goes ahead with his own meal, and one is hungry and another is drunk. What! Do you not have houses to eat and drink in? Or do you despise the church of God and humiliate those who have nothing? What shall I say to you? Shall I com-

mend you in this? No, I will not. For I received from the Lord what I also delivered to you, that the Lord Jesus on the night when he was betrayed took bread, and when he had given thanks, he broke it, and said, "This is my body which is for you. Do this in remembrance of me." In the same way also the cup, after supper, saying, "This cup is the new covenant in my blood. Do this, as often as you drink it, in remembrance of me." For as often as you eat this bread and drink the cup, you proclaim the Lord's death until he comes.

Our eating with our Lord is not different from our learning to be his disciples, his holy people. The kind of holiness that marks the church, however, is not that of moral perfection, but the holiness of a people who have learned not to fear one another and thus are capable of love. We do not just go ahead with our own meals, or our lives, but have learned to live in the presence of others without fear and envy. We thus become a perfect people through the meal we share with our Lord. We learn that forgiveness of the enemy, even when the enemy is ourselves, is the way God would have his kingdom accomplished.

In his illuminating book about his missionary work with the Masai, Vincent Donovan powerfully illustrates the inherent relation between our holiness as a people and our eucharistic celebrations. One of the most significant gestures for the Masai is to offer one another a handful of grass as a sign of peace, happiness, and well-being. During arguments, for example, a tuft of grass might be offered by one Masai to another as an assurance that no violence would erupt because of the argument. "No Masai would violate that sacred sign of peace offered, because it was not only a sign of peace; it was peace."[12]

Donovan describes how the beginning of a mass among the Masai would involve the whole village as every activity of the village, from praying for the sick to dancing, would become a natural part of the mass. Yet he says he never knew if the eucharist would emerge from all this. The leaders of the village were the ones to decide yes or no.

If there had been selfishness and forgetfulness and hatefulness and lack of forgiveness in the work that had been done, in the life that had been led here, let them not make a sacrilege out of it by calling it the Body of Christ. And the leaders did decide occasionally that, despite the prayers and readings and discussions, if the grass had stopped, if someone, or some group, in the village had refused to accept the grass as the sign of the peace of Christ, there would be no eucharist at this time.[13]

The Masai understand well the relation between their eucharistic celebration and the demand to be a holy people, a peaceable people. For the eucharist and their baptism are not isolated acts separate from the kind of people they are meant to be. Rather the eucharist is possible because they have become what they, and we, were meant to be: a people capable of passing grass, of forgiveness, in a world that would have us believe that human relations are ultimately determined by manipulation and violence.

5. THE SOCIAL ETHICS OF THE CHURCH

It may be objected that all this still remains very abstract. Even if it is true that the church itself is a social ethic, surely it must also have a social ethic that reaches out in strategic terms in the societies in which it finds itself. That is certainly the case, but a social ethic in this latter sense cannot be done in the abstract. For there is no universal social strategy of the church that applies equally to diverse social circumstances. Indeed, different circumstances and social contexts bring different needs and strategies. For example, the church's stance in the context of totalitarian governments is obviously different than its stance in liberal democratic regimes.

Yet this does not mean the church must have a theory of government peculiar to itself that can help it understand the different ways it must respond to totalitarian regimes in contrast to the more liberal democratic type. The contemporary church has too often assumed that we must naturally favor "democratic" societies because such societies have institutionalized the freedom of religion through legal recognition of the freedom of conscience. As Christians we should be particularly sensitive to the misleading assumption that democracies are intrinsically more just because they provide more freedom than other kinds of societies. Freedom is an abstraction that can easily direct our attention away from faithfully serving as the church in democratic social orders. The crucial question is what kind of freedom and what do we wish to do with it.

Yet it may be suggested that even if there is no one theory of government intrinsic to the church's self-understanding, surely there are some values, which may have diverse institutional forms, that the church has a stake in promoting. For example, Enda McDonagh speaks of "kingdom values," such as freedom, inviolability of the person, and equality as necessary correlatives of the Christian commitment. Indeed the promotion of these values in wider society is entailed by the Christian duty to promote more nearly just social orders. Christians, according to McDonagh, support these "values" as intrinsic to the kingdom, but they are not peculiar to Christians *per se*. Rather the pursuit of justice

> not only allows for cooperation with the non-believer, it opens up the non-believer and believer to an awareness of the human, the mystery of the human. . . . In this way the discernment and promotion of social justice provides a pedagogy of the faith, a learning experience that has the capacity, under the attracting power of the self-giving and revealing God whom we are encountering in the neighbor, to be transcended into explicit recognition of God, into faith. Not only does faith demand social justice, social justice finally demands faith—for the believer, increases in faith.[14]

It is extremely interesting to compare McDonagh's position in this respect with that of Yoder. For Yoder says,

> The ultimate and most profound reason to consider Christ— rather than democracy or justice, or equality or liberty—as the hope of the world, is not the negative observation, clear enough already, that hopes of this kind generally remain incomplete and disappointing, or that they can lead those who trust them to pride or brutality. The fundamental limitation of these hopes is found in the fact that in their search for power and in the urgency with which they seek to guarantee justice they are still not powerful enough. They locate the greatest need of man in the wrong place. . . . Those for whom Jesus Christ is the hope of the world will for this reason not measure their contemporary social involvement by its efficacy for tomorrow nor by its success in providing work, or freedom, or food or in building new social structures, but by identifying with the Lord in whom they have placed their trust.[15]

Yoder is not objecting to McDonagh's concern for justice, nor does he wish to deny that God requires that we seek justice for all people. His question is, what is meant by justice and how is it related to our understanding of Jesus' proclamation of the kingdom? Once "justice" is made a criterion of Christian social strategy, it can too easily take on a meaning and life of its own that is not informed by the Christian's fundamental convictions. It can, for example, be used to justify the Christian's resort to violence to secure a more "relative justice." But then we must ask if this is in fact the justice we are to seek as Christians.

Put differently, the problem with identifying, or at least closely associating, the meaning of the gospel with the pursuit of "kingdom values" such as freedom and equality is that such values lack the concreteness, the material content, of the kingdom as found in Jesus' life and death. It is not sufficient to interpret, as McDonagh does, the eschatological nature of freedom and equality by noting that they are ideals never fully realized.[16] The problem is not that the kingdom brought by Christ is too idealistic to be realized. The problem is just the opposite. The kingdom is present in Jesus Christ. It is thus the ultimate realism that calls into question our vague ideals of freedom, equality, and peace. We do not learn what the kingdom is by learning of freedom and equality; we must first experience the kingdom if we are to know what kind of freedom and what kind of equality we should desire. Our freedom is that of service, and our equality is that before God, and neither can be achieved through the coercive efforts of idealists who would transform the world in their image.

Put in terms that have now become familiar, freedom and equality are not self-interpreting, but require a tradition to give them content. For example, it is a truism of political theory that freedom of the individual and a more egalitarian society are not consistent ideals—that is, the pursuit of equality necessarily will qualify someone's sense of what it means to be "free." Indeed, I suspect that our current concentration on these two "values" may be deeply distorting for the appropriate aims of a good society. Each of them, in our current situation, tends to underwrite a view of society as essentially a collection of individuals who are engaged in continual bargaining procedures to provide mutual security without letting it cost too much in their personal freedom. Questions of the common purpose of such societies simply cannot be asked. Distinctions between society and state, while perfectly intelligible in a formal mode, make little empirical sense, because "society" lacks a sufficient narrative to give it moral substance. The church, to be sure, has a stake in a "limited state," but what keeps the state limited is not finally a theory about the place of the state within society but a people who have the power of discernment and know when to say "no."[17]

Thus to say that the church must pursue societal justice is certainly right, but it is not very informative. For justice needs to be displayed and imaginatively construed by a people who have been formed to know that genuine justice derives from our receiving what is not due us. Such people serve the cause of justice best by exemplifying in their own lives how to help one another—i.e., how goods might be shared since no one has a rightful claim on them. For there can be no justice where there is no sense of what things are rightly desired. Otherwise justice remains formal and procedural. Of course there is much to be said for procedural norms, but they can never be sufficient to sustain the conversation necessary for a people to survive as a good people.

Moreover when freedom and equality are made ideal abstractions, they become the justification for violence, since if these values are absent or insufficiently institutionalized some conclude they must be forced into existence. As McDonagh points out, "most political orders are established by violence and certainly use violence to maintain themselves."[18] This is not without ethical justification, since, as McDonagh suggests, the state's hegemony of violence is at least in principle rooted in the just war rationale. The state uses violence to restrain those who have no respect for the lives and rights of other people in that society. Thus it seems the state can claim to use violence as the necessary means to preserve freedom and justice. And by further inference of this reasoning, when freedom and justice are missing the Christian can resort to violence so that they may be achieved.

No one can easily dismiss the power of this position. Moreover, it certainly makes clear that the question of violence is the central issue for any Christian social ethic. Can Christians ever be justified in resorting to arms to do "some good"? Are Christians not unjust if they allow another person to be injured or even killed if they might prevent that by the use of violence? Indeed should not Christians call on the power of the state to employ its coercive force to secure more relative forms of justice? Such action would not be a question of using violence to be "in control," but simply to prevent a worse evil.

Although I have sympathy with this position and though it certainly cannot be discounted as a possibility for Christians, the problem with these attempts to commit the Christian to limited use of violence is that they too often distort the character of our alternatives. Violence used in the name of justice, or freedom, or equality is seldom simply a matter of justice—it is a matter of the power of some over others. Moreover, when violence is justified in principle as a necessary strategy for securing justice, it stills the imaginative search for nonviolent ways of resistance to injustice.[19] For true justice never comes through violence, nor can it be based on violence. It can only be based on truth, which has no need to resort to violence to secure its own existence. Such a justice comes at best fitfully to nation states, for by nature we are people who fear disorder and violence and thus we prefer order (even if the order is built on the lies inspired by our hates, fears, and resentments) to truth. The Church, therefore, as a community based on God's kingdom of truth cannot help but make all rulers tremble, especially when those rulers have become "the people."

7. Casuistry as a Narrative Art

1. NARRATIVE, VIRTUES, AND CASUISTRY

I have argued that the question "What ought I to be?" precedes the question "What ought I to do?" If we begin our ethical reflection with the latter question we stand the risk of misunderstanding how practical reason should work as well as the moral life itself. For the question "What ought I to do?" tempts us to assume that moral situations are abstracted from the kind of people and history we have come to be. But that simply is not the case. The "situations" we confront are such only because we are first a certain kind of people. In fact, the very idea that ethics should be primarily concerned with "quandaries" and the kind of decisions we ought to make about them reflects our current understanding of ourselves as a people without a history. "Situations" are not "out there" waiting to be seen but are created by the kind of people we are.

For example, there is a tribe of people in Africa called the Nuer.[1] These are good people who have a strong sense of communal care for one another. Moreover they are generally a gentle people, at peace with themselves and their neighbors. However they have the view that any of their children born obviously retarded or deformed is not a Nuer. Instead they think such a child is a hippopotamus. An elaborate mythology, in which the various kinds of animals have their place and responsibilities, underwrites this belief. The Nuer do not have a well-defined concept of "human being" or "animal," but they recognize differences in roles. In particular, they feel strongly that each type of creature is best cared for by its own kind. Therefore a deformed child is placed in the river to be cared for by its own — namely hippopotami. From our perspective this is child euthanasia, but the Nuer feel they are doing the only thing they can do if they are to act responsibly. For them a "quandary" would be raised if the mother of such a child decided she was so attached to this "hippopotamus" that she wanted to keep it.

Such an example does not show, as many assume, that all moral judgments are "relative." Rather it shows that the kind of quandaries we confront depend on the kind of people we are and the way we have learned to construe the world through our language, habits, and feelings.[2] If it is true that I can act only in the world I see and that my seeing is a matter of my learning to say, it is equally the case that my "saying" requires sustained habits that form my emotions and passions, teaching me to feel one way rather than another. We are therefore quite right to think that questions of feeling are central for determining what I ought to do since they are signals that help remind us what kind of people we are.

The question of what I ought to *do* is actually about what I am or ought to be. "Should I or should I not have an abortion?" is not just a question about an "act" but about what kind of person I am going to be. Too often we forget that the very description of an act as "abortion" reflects a moral tradition with certain presuppositions — for instance, not only that life is God's gift but also that children are important for the tradition's continuing journey. We tend to overlook the significance of such suppositions and take for granted that they are written into the way things are and thus cannot be lost. In fact, however, they require constant reappropriation by a people through positive commitments to having children and the protection of life. These particular commitments are not the only ones entering into the question of what we should do in a specific case, but they are necessary background for assessing the meaning of abortion and why it is generally prohibited. However, it may be true that we are no longer a people with such positive commitments and thus the prohibition against abortion is not intelligible. If that is the case, we must recognize that we have not simply changed our minds about a particular act called abortion, but by changing our understanding or eliminating our notion of abortion we have in fact changed ourselves.

Notions like "abortion" are not simply given; their meaning and intelligibility depend on a narrative construal. Indeed part of the problem with the "old morality," particularly in Catholic moral theology, was its concentration on "act descriptions" as representing an "objective and thus universal morality." Those "descriptions," however, were abstracted from the communal narratives and practices which made them compelling. As a result, it was forgotten that "abortion" is not merely a description of a set of facts, but a mode of construing the world correlative to a people's convictions.

But this way of putting the matter can be misleading if it is assumed that we start out with a set of basic moral convictions from which we learn that certain kinds of behavior are right or wrong. Indeed that is just the kind of mistake involved in the attempt to demonstrate the rightness or wrongness of certain actions abstracted from their narrative context. For example, most people concerned about abortion would say that what is wrong with abortion is the violation of some basic principle such as "life is sacred," or "it is wrong to take life directly." Thus it appears that the prohibition against abortion is a deduction from a yet more basic principle. The debate then revolves around the issue of whether the deduction is valid, whether a fetus in fact has the characteristics of a human being capable of possessing "rights."

There is no question of the rational power of this model of moral reflection, but it is my contention that it is seriously flawed. It is not that I disagree with the principles stated here in themselves but I do disagree with how we come to them and make them our own and how they work in our lives. Such an account fails to do justice to the connection between the stories that form our lives and the prohibitions and positive commitments correlative to those stories. What must be seen is that the virtues and the rules constituting a morality are community dependent.

For example MacIntryre asks us to

> imagine a community which has come to recognize that there is a good for man and that this good is such that it can only be achieved in and through the life of a community constituted by this shared project. We can envision such a community requiring two distinct types of precepts to be observed in order to ensure the requisite kind of order for its common life. The first would be a set of precepts enjoining the virtues, those dispositions without the exercise of which the good cannot be achieved, more particularly if the good is a form of life which includes as an essential part the exercise of the virtues. The second would be a set of precepts prohibiting those actions destructive of those human relationships which are necessary to a community in which and for which the good is to be achieved and for which the virtues are to be practiced. Both sets of precepts derive their point, purpose, and justification from the *telos*, but in two very different ways. To violate the second type of precept is to com-

mit an act sufficiently intolerable to exclude oneself from that community in which alone one can hope to achieve the good. Thus the absolute prohibition of certain specifiable kinds of actions finds a necessary place within a certain type of teleological framework.[3]

Putting MacIntyre's point in the language I have been using, certain prohibitions of a community are such that to violate them means that one is no longer leading one's life in terms of the narrative that forms that community's understanding of its basic purpose. For the *telos* in fact is a narrative, and the good is not so much a clearly defined "end" as it is a sense of the journey on which that community finds itself. In political terms it means that the conversation of community is not *about* some good still to be realized, but the conversation *is* the good insofar as it is through the conversation that the community keeps faithful to the narrative.

A community's moral prohibitions, therefore, are not so much "derived" from basic principles as they exhibit the way the community discovers what its habits and commitments entail. You do not first have the principle "life is sacred" and then deduce that abortion is wrong. Rather you learn about the value of life, and in particular human life that comes in the form of our children, because your community and your parents acting on behalf of your community, do not practice abortion. Therefore the negative prohibitions of a community though they often appear to apply to anyone because of their minimal character (e.g., do not murder) in fact gain their intelligibility from that community's more substantive and positive practices. Prohibitions are the markers for the outer limits of the communal self-understandings. In short, they tell us that if we do this or no longer disapprove of that, we will no longer be living out the tradition that originally formed us.

The stories that comprise a living tradition, if they are serious, are meant to tell us the way things are—that is, we learn from them the conditions of truth. Reexamining the prohibitions required by particular narratives is one of the ways the narratives are tested against our ongoing experience. In this way the narrative is challenged and renewed. For example, the current abortion controversy is not simply a question of the permissibility of abortion. If it can be shown that Christians have been wrong to prohibit abortion and yet that prohibition is in fact integral to Christian convictions, it follows that there is something basically wrong with how Christians understand the nature of human existence. On the other hand, a moral crisis may suggest that a community has not rightly understood the practical force of its own convictions.

This kind of testing can be construed as a way of showing that some kind of natural law assumptions, at least in a qualified form, are integral to Christian ethics. For "natural law" really names those moral convictions that have been tested by the experiences of the Christian community and have been judged essential for sustaining its common life. However Christian convictions must remain open to challenge from sources outside the Christian community, since those convictions presuppose that this is God's world—e.g., Christians may well learn from other traditions that our attempt to justify violence in the interest of protecting the innocent is finally self-contradictory. Yet the process may also work the other way. Thus our culture's current acceptance of abortion as morally acceptable may be shown to be "unnatural" if we are also to continue to be a people who will bring children into the world and to care for them. It may not be possible at certain times to persuade others that such is the case, but that does not mean the question involved is any the less one of truth—that is, a question about the shape and nature of our lives appropriate to living in a world created by a gracious God.

What I mean by casuistry, then, is not just the attempt to adjudicate difficult cases of conscience within a system of moral principles, but is the process by which a tradition tests whether its practices are consistent (that is, truthful) or inconsistent in the light of its basic habits and convictions or whether these convictions require new practices and behavior. In fact a tradition often does not understand the implications of its basic convictions. Those implications become apparent only through the day-to-day living of a people pledged to embody that narrative within their own lives. There is a sense, therefore, in which we rightly discover that to which we are deeply committed only by having our lives challenged by others. That challenge does not come exclusively from without, however, but is entailed as well by the narrative that has captured our lives. We thus confront certain dangers and challenges, or perhaps better, we only recognize certain dangers and challenges because we have been trained to do so by the narrative that has bound our lives. It is true that in the beginning we perhaps do not recognize such dangers to be part of the narrative but as we "grow into the story" we see more fully its implications. Casuistry is the reflection by a community on its experience to test imaginatively the often unnoticed and unacknowledged implications of its narrative commitments.

Perhaps I can make this clearer by calling attention to the paradoxical truism that the brave necessarily know fears that cowards never experience. For if the brave know not fear, if the brave know not how much they risk by being brave, then they cannot be brave. Some, to be sure, may appear brave, and at times we cannot tell the difference between the persons of courage and the foolhardy, but if they know not fear they cannot be courageous. That is why one action, no matter how dramatic, is not sufficient to attribute virtue, for to be virtuous requires that we be capable of sustaining a perduring project. For example, it is only the courageous who can refuse to resort too quickly to force in resolving disputes, since they know that their courage must be tempered by patience. They may rightly fear the loss of the esteem of others for what may appear their hesitancy, but that is integral to being courageous. By being brave we necessarily risk being exposed to dangers the coward or the foolhearty cannot know and even we cannot always anticipate, but we know that nonetheless we must be courageous if we are to rightfully live out the story of the savior who would not have his kingdom established through violence.

Casuistry, therefore, cannot be limited simply to consideration of "cases" or situations, but also requires the imaginative testing of our habits of life against the well-lived and virtuous lives of others. It is from such testing that we learn what kinds of situations we may well have to anticipate as entailed by the narrative and community of which we are a part. Attending to such lives does not mean that we try to imitate others, though certainly imitation may be useful, but by letting those lives form our own we learn what our particular way of embodying the story entails.[4] We cannot learn the story by doing exactly what others did, for we cannot do exactly what they did. Rather, we must let their lives imaginatively challenge our own, so that we may learn how to embody the virtues which determined not only what they did, but how they did it.

2. DECISIONS, DECISIONS, DECISIONS!

It may be objected that this approach to ethics nevertheless fails to come to grips with the real challenges of the moral life. It is all well and good to emphasize the narrative form of our moral convictions, the necessity of the virtues as the background to our decisions. However we must still make decisions. Nothing has been said about knowing which decisions we ought or ought not to make or how they can be justified. Classical issues such as the significance of consequences and the absoluteness of certain rules have not been addressed.

We have to make decisions and we have to know better how to reason about them. We decide to marry or not. We decide whether to remain married or not. We decide to have or not have children. We may have to decide whether or not to have an abortion, whether or not to obey the law requiring all eighteen-year-olds to register for the draft. We have to decide whether to become a lawyer or a businessman. We have to decide whether to lie, tell the truth, or equivocate when a terminally ill person asks if he is dying. We have to decide if it is permissible to withhold some life-sustaining therapies from children suffering from debilitating birth defects. We have to decide whether to put more funds into cancer research than into aid for the deaf and blind. We have to decide whether to put more resources into medicine aimed at crisis intervention for particular patients or to emphasize nutritional programs that will benefit more people.

The emphasis on the narrative context of moral reflection and virtues as the necessary basis for our decisions simply does not seem to help us answer these questions—which we suspect are the real center of the moral life. It is all very well to say that "decisions are what we make when everything else has been lost,"[5] but clever rhetoric finally cannot distract us from the real issues. No matter what narrative we find ourselves in or what virtues we have acquired, we do find ourselves having to make choices that require justification. "Quandary ethics" may have overlooked the significance of character and virtue for the moral life, but emphasis on the latter cannot relieve us from the need to justify our moral decisions in a consistent and nonarbitrary manner.

Indeed total emphasis on narrative and virtue may seem to invite just such arbitrariness. For when it comes to decisions, such an ethic seems ultimately to assume some form of intuition to justify individuals' perceptions of what they should do given their "story" and corresponding virtues. What is lacking is any public criteria for the testing of such decisions. Therefore the emphasis on the virtues, in spite of denials to the contrary, remains an irreducibly subjective account. Some account of rules and the status of consequences cannot be avoided if we are to make sense of the full spectrum of our moral experience and in particular our moral decisions.

Such a challenge is obviously serious and significant for the kind of position I have tried to develop. Yet I think that I am not short of a response. There is nothing about an emphasis on narrative and the virtues that in itself denies that we must still make decisions or that we are often rightly required to justify why we have acted as we have. However, it is true that those decisions do not have the same status they assume in ethics that ignore the significance of the virtues. For at least part of the intention of an ethics of virtue is to free us from the assumption of the felt "necessities" and "givens" we too often accept as part of our decisions. We often do not have to decide, at least not in the way assumed.

For example, those who identify with a nonviolent stance are often challenged with "But what would you do if . . . ?" The dots are usually filled in with a description of a case where it seems absolutely essential, and certainly for the greatest good, to use rather than refrain from violence. Such cases are usually enough to convince others that nonviolence simply cannot be justified as an unqualified principle. It seems self-evident that violence at times is necessary. Of course everybody assumes that it is always better to avoid the use of force if possible, but it seems that something is decisively wrong with any ethic that rules our the legitimate or even tragic use of violence before the fact. Yet that seemingly self-evident presupposition ironically contains a deterministic view of our existence that I expect few of us would be willing to accept. For it is my contention that if we are genuinely non-violent we can no more decide to use violence even if the situation seems to warrant it, than the courageous can decide, under certain conditions, to be cowardly.

For as John Howard Yoder has pointed out, the challenge "What would you do if . . . ?" assumes a relationship between persons that is mechanistic:

> if I turn the machine one way it will follow one course inevitably, if I push a different set of buttons the machine will clearly operate in another direction. It is assumed that I am the only party making decisions in the total process. The attacker is so pre-programmed that he will not be making any more decisions. His only desire is like an automaton to do the worst evil he can, or the particular evil he has fixed his mind on. Nor are there elsewhere in the total situation other persons whose actions might get in the way of the outworking of the mechanism, which I am therefore solely responsible to steer.[6]

Once such a determined course is set, violence certainly becomes the only alternative — it is a self-fulfilling prophecy. But that does not have to be the case. What such an example suggests, and it is just as true of cases that do not raise directly the question of violence, is that too often to ask "What should I decide under X or Y conditions?" or "How can what I decided be justified?" is an attempt to still the imagination by accepting the "necessities" of certain descriptions. Moreover, those "necessities" too often simply assume that among the givens are my limits or the limits of my community, and never think of suggesting ways in which the community and myself might be asked to change our lives.

For example, arguments for the permissibility of abortion often turn on cases of twelve-year-old girls who have become pregnant through rape or incest. The question "What would you do?" in such a circumstance seems immediately to suggest that we ought to approve of an abortion as the least evil thing to do for such a misfortunate young girl. I am not here attempting to argue that abortion might not be a viable alternative in such a situation; I simply want to note that the reason abortion seems to be the *only* alternative in such a situation is partly because of the kind of society in which we live and the kind of people we are. The "necessity" of abortion in such circumstances too often is the necessity generated by our unwillingness to change our lives to any signficant degree so that another alternative might be contemplated.

Or again Yoder reminds us that most scenarios that begin with "What would you do if . . . ?" also assume that my righteousness and my welfare are the overriding considerations. Or I might say I can contemplate sacrificing my welfare in order not to use violence, but I cannot contemplate sacrificing the welfare of others for whom I am responsible — e.g., my wife or my child. Yet what I am ultimately defending is not really the innocent neighbor in the form of my wife or child, but I am defending what is mine.[7] To recognize this does not mean that I should not defend my wife and child, but it does put the issue in a different frame. For as Yoder suggests, it is not a foregone conclusion for Christianity, as it is for ethical systems which locate value in the self and its relations, that defense of the victim is overriding. "Christianity relativizes the value of self and survival as it affirms the dignity of the enemy and offender. In the face of this specific Christian claim, what seems *prima facie* evident becomes arguable."[8]

This point reminds us that the description under which the decision is proposed is as important as the decision itself. For the description frames the decision. The truth behind the claim that "decision is what we do when everything else has been lost" is that decisions we seemed "forced to make" are in fact those for which we have no satisfactory description. But what does it mean to say that we have no satisfactory description? I suggest it means that we have no satisfactory way of understanding them as part of the ongoing narrative of myself or my community. They thus become significant not because they are "what I am really about morally," but because they do not represent what I am really about. Morally the most important things about us are those matters about which we never have to make a "decision." Thus nonviolent persons do not have to choose to use or not to use violence, but rather their being nonviolent means they must use their imaginations to form their whole way of life consistent with their convictions.

So it turns out that narrative does have more to do with "decisions" than most anticipate. For the abstraction of "decisions" or "acts" into "case studies" which are then to be adjudicated in terms of overriding "principles" justified either in a deontological or consequential manner fails to deal with the most essential aspect of any decision—namely its narrative context. The descriptions of "situations" do not come as givens, but are parts of a larger narrative whole. Our "freedom" in regard to our decisions depends exactly on not having to accept the determinism of those who would encourage us to assume that we have to "make" a "decision" because "this is the way things are." Such determinism can be defeated only if we have the descriptive skills provided by a truthful narrative to see the "situation" in a new light—that is, in a light that enables us to do what we do or not do in a manner consistent with our moral commitments.

For example, Yoder asks us to consider the actual options connected with the question, "What would you do if . . . ?" The first option has a tragic outcome since the attacker would be able to carry out his or her evil design. Second, there is the possibility of martyrdom for either the victim or myself. For Yoder reminds us that "Christians have held that the death of a Christian believer, as a result of his behaving in a Christian way at the hands of the agents of evil, can become through no merit of his or her own a special witness and a monument of the power of God. The death of that Christian disciple makes a greater contribution to the cause of God and to the welfare of the world than his staying alive at the cost of killing would have done. For ever after it is looked on with respect. Why not accept suffering? Jesus did."[9]

Third, there is the option that looks for a way out. This might come in several forms as a "natural" way out, such as a loving gesture might, even if it is unlikely, disarm the attacker emotionally. Or there might be a "providential" way out, assuming that whatever

happens will work for the "good for them that love the Lord." Finally, there is the option of killing the attacker, which must also include
the possibility that I try to kill him or her but fail.

By spelling out the options in this manner, Yoder means to
enliven our imaginations, to free us from our assumptions schooled
on the presumption of the necessity of violence, to show that it is
"logically preposterous" to assume that in such situations we can only
choose between the first and fourth options. As soon as one takes in-
ventory of the many variables at work, the proposed violent intervention loses its self-evidence.

> Certainly for anyone standing within that particular stream of
> human history which we call the Christian Church it must be
> denied that death is the greatest evil which one can suffer, since
> a believer's death for a reason relating to God's will and His way
> is a part of His victory over evil within this world, so that the
> acceptance of suffering is not unthinkable. Certainly anyone
> whose vision of the drama of human conflict is deeper than that
> of the television western has some awareness of the complexity
> of historical causality and some notion of how seldom things
> turn out the way men have predicted, especially when what they
> have been predicting is wholesome fruit to be borne by
> violence. Thus the unforeseen creative solution clearly belongs
> in the picture. . . .
>
> To state the matter more broadly, especially as it is made
> to apply to the case of war: by assuming that it is my business
> to prevent or to bring judgment upon evil, I authorize myself
> to close the door upon the possibilities of reconciling and heal-
> ing. When I take it into my own hands to guarantee that events
> will not turn out in a way that is painful or disadvantageous to
> me, or illegal, I close off the live possibilities of reconciliation
> which might have been let loose in the world.[10]

Yoder also defends the notion of "providence" as crucial for
justifying nonviolence. By providence he does not mean the illusory
notion that "everything will come out all right in the end," nor that
it is the duty of every individual to make history come out right.
Rather, the notion of providence "designates the conviction that the
events of history are under control in ways that are beyond both our
discerning and our manipulating, although their pattern may occasionally be perceived by the prophet, and later will be celebrated by
the community."[11] Yoder notes that such a position might well be
supported by a decent humanism embodied in the maxim "if you

have a choice between a real evil and a hypothetical evil, always take the hypothetical one." Yet there are also specifically Christian reasons for taking this perspective, not the least of which is that Christian love requires us to go beyond the bounds of decent humanism by making the enemy, not just the object of reciprocal love, but a "positively privileged object of love."[12]

Moreover, committed Christians see their faith not first of all as an

> ethical stance about which they want to be consistent, a set of rules they want to be sure not to break; but a gracious privilege which they want to share. They guide their lives not so much by "How can I avoid doing wrong?" or even "How can I do the right?" as by "How can I be a reconciling presence in the life of my neighbor?" From this perspective I might justify firm non-violent restraint, but certainly never killing. Most of the time the committed Christian testifies in theory that God intervenes in the lives of selfish creatures to change those lives and that he does so through his children; when is that testimony tested if not now, when I am invited to act toward this aggressor on the assumption that there can be for him no change of heart?[13]

The final justification of such a stance, particularly if it results in martyrdom, is that it is simply

> to share in God's way with His world. How then could I possibly be led along the path of innocent suffering, which the New Testament and much later Christian testimony indicate is in some sense a normal one for at least some Christians to need to follow at least sometimes, if in my pragmatic managing of the situation I have excluded this as the one thing that must not happen?[14]

Of course we must make decisions. Of course we will be forced to make many decisions that we would prefer to avoid. Yet by noting the narrative context that all such decisions assume, but which is often not made explicit, we see better the crucial question is how that "decision" is to be understood. By calling attention to Yoder's analysis of the challenge of "What would you do if . . . ?" to those who have a commitment to nonviolence I have tried to show that the crucial question is not an abstract analysis of the "situation" in terms of one or another option of normative ethical theory, but how we are to understand such challenges within a narrative framework. For Yoder's appeal to "providence" in fact offers a way of "reading" such situations in a manner that "fits" within the continuing story of a community's life with God. It is not, therefore a blind or unwarranted faith that everything will work out in the end. On the contrary, it is a strong rational claim that our existence is bounded by a truth that will have its way with us as truth must — that is, by defeating the violent with the power of unrelenting love. God's story cannot be defeated by our attempts to become the authors of this world's narrative by employing violent means.

From this perspective I think it can be seen why Christians have been tempted to approach the problem of "decision making" and justification in deontological terms. For there is a sense in which they must act faithful to the story regardless of the consequences. Let justice be done, let truth be told, do the right regardless of who is hurt or the tragedies caused, for that is what our God requires. But such an emphasis can become merely a formula for moral callousness and self-righteousness if it is divorced from the narrative context that makes it intelligible. For it is not simply a matter of "let justice be done" but of the kind of justice and by whom and how it is done. It is not just a matter of "let the truth be told" but what truth is and how it is told in love. Yes, dying persons should know they are dying, but they should also be given the assurance that they will not be abandoned by us in that truth.

But Christians have also been attracted by, and used, forms of consequential reasoning to inform their decisions. The very concern to do the best thing, "under the circumstances," and to serve the neighbor beyond the requirements of duty seems to require that we attend to the effects of our actions. Yet again the isolation of "consequences" as the determining factor in our decisions invites a sense of control and omnipotence that is not easily justified. Arguments for the "greatest good" or "lesser evil" are too abstract, as they far too easily accept the "necessities" of our existence as a given. As a result, we lose our imaginative power to offer the world a new possibility by being a different kind of people. To be sure, the narrative of the Christian people requires us to look to the good that we should do or the evil we should prevent, but such a good and such an evil must not be constrained by an imagination which assumes that the "effectiveness" the world desires is our last word. For we know that by nature we are not violent, by nature we are not liars, by nature we seek not injustice. Christians therefore cannot be content with a morality that accepts sin as a given. It is our task to call ourselves and others to be true to ourselves as God's creatures.

Once we resist the temptation to abstract "situations" and "cases" from their narrative context, we can begin to appreciate the testimony of many, both Christians and non-Christians, that in matters of significance even involving the "hardest choices" there was no "decision" to be made. Rather, the decision makes itself if we know who we are and what is required of us. Thomas More did not choose to die at the hands of Henry. He did everything he could to avoid having Henry put him to death, not only for his own sake but also because he wished to spare Henry from that task. But he could not take the oath of succession and as a result he had to die. He did not understand that he had thereby made a "decision" needing justification, deontologically or consequentially. He simply did what he had to do.[15]

But such dramatic examples may well be misleading, for our lives are not made up of such dramatic confrontations, although they are no less constituted by such commitments. Those committed to living faithfully do not have to decide constantly whether to be faithful or not. They simply are faithful. That does not mean that they will not be tempted, but even such temptation does not so much require a decision as it denotes an alternative that, although present, is not a real possibility. It is not a real possibility because it would change their lives, which is but another way of saying it would change how they have to tell their story.

It is interesting to note how much of the discussion dealing with "decisions," and their justification involves questions of sexual relations. It is as though our sexual relations were a matter of constant decisions. If that is the case we are indeed in a fine mess, for if there is anything we need freedom from it is the need to make constant decisions about whether to be sexually faithful or not.

For example, I have a friend who travels a great deal. Anyone who travels knows that there is something inherently tempting about getting on airplanes and going places where you are not known well. The experience conveys a freedom that might allow a casual sexual engagement where no strings are attached or any consequences ever follow. My friend, who confesses he often enjoys fantasizing in such a manner, was once taken aback when while he was on an almost empty plane returning to his home a stewardess actually proposed that they might enjoy one another's company for awhile. My friend candidly admits that the first thing that occurred to him was not the rule "Thou shalt not commit adultery" but, "How could I explain to my wife why I was late?" But that question was enough for him to refuse the offer, because it occurred to him he would have to lie, and while he might even have thought up a good lie, he simply did not want to have to begin that kind of life.

That lie, which admittedly would not have been any more significant than the casual sexual affair, would have changed who he was. In refusing the stewardess he did not feel as if he had made a "decision"; the decision had already been made by the kind of person he was and the kind of life he had with his family.[16] Indeed, all the "decision" did was make him aware of what he already was, since he really did not know that he had developed the habit of faithfulness. I expect that many of our decisions are of this sort. We tend to think of them as "decisions," when in fact they are but confirmation of what we have become without realizing it.

That recognition, of course, works as much negatively as it does positively. We may discover our "unfaithfulness" by our needing to make a decision at all. Or in regard to violence, we seldom recognize how deeply filled with hate, resentment, and violence we are. Often this is true of those who are pledged to be nonviolent, as their explicit commitment may be a strategy for gaining power over others in the name of moral righteousness. That such is the case merely reminds us why we so desperately need a community capable of challenging our self-absorption by calling into question our presumed rational justification of our behavior.

3. CASUISTRY, CHOICES, AND THE CHURCH

One of the difficulties of casuistry in its traditional mode, or as it takes the form of "normative theory" in a more secular context, is its implicit individualistic presumptions. It is as if the individual simply bumps up against decisions devoid of any communal context. But we know that any decision we make involves others, not simply in the sense of harm or benefit, but we affect how others understand themselves and their relationship to us and God. Indeed the primary task of casuistry is to help us understand our interconnectedness so that we can better appreciate how what we do not only fits within the story of our lives, but also how it is determined by and determines the ongoing story of the Christian community.

Though currently casuistry is regarded with a good deal of suspicion as a minimalist endeavor to evade some of the more onerous obligations of a legalistic ethic, no community can or should try to avoid developing a tradition of moral testing embodying the wisdom of that community concerning sets of issues peculiar to its nature. The question is not whether to have or not to have casuistry, but what kind we should have. This is particularly the case among Christians, since the very nature of our convictions makes problematic any account of a self-centered decision-making process. As Yoder reminds us,

> Whereas common sense tells us that people tend to be selfish and that this tends to influence their perception of things, Christian faith goes further. It warns me in particular that I use my self-centered control of my decisions as a tool of my rebelliousness, as a way of solidifying my independence from my Maker. Christian thought labels as "pride" that rebellious autonomy which I insist on despite the fact that ultimately, if not overcome by His grace, it means my own destruction. Common sense says that any person is limited in his capacity to observe and evaluate the facts by his particular point of view and the limits of his vision; but Christian faith tells me that my selfish mind, my impatient and retaliating spirit, and my adrenalin positively warp the way I perceive the facts in order to make them reflections of my self-esteem and my desire to be independent of my Creator and of my neighbor. Thus while common sense argues for modesty about my capacity to make a valid decision all by myself, the Christian understanding of sin calls for me to repent of the very idea that I might make a decision completely on my own.
>
> The real temptation of good people like us is not the crude and the crass and the carnal, as those traits were defined in popular puritanism. The really refined temptation with which Jesus himself was tried was not crude sensuality but that of egocentric altruism; of being oneself the incarnation of a good and righteous cause for which others may rightly be made to suffer; of stating in the form of a duty to others one's self-justification.[17]

Casuistry, at least in a Christian context, is not just a possibility but a necessity, because it provides the means by which we learn to check our own particular rendering of the story of God with that of our community. The church not only is, but must be, a "community of moral discourse"—that is, a community that sustains a rigorous analysis of the implications of its commitments across generations as it faces new challenges and situations.[18] For as I suggested above, as a people, often we do not understand the implications of the narrative that gives us our being. The church is that community pledged constantly to work out and test the implications of the story of God, as known through Israel and Jesus Christ, for its common life as well as the life of the world.

There is no assurance that this "working out" will always be faithful to the kind of discipleship required by Jesus. For example, it may well be that the development of the "just war" theory, which was certainly an imaginative attempt to maintain the gospel's commitments to forgiveness and peacemaking and yet respond to the Christian's increasing responsibility to wider society, was a mistake. Or it may be that the prohibition against remarriage after a "divorce" was more rigorous than it needed to be to maintain the Christian commitment to fidelity in marriage. Such matters often are not apparent at once, but depend on the working out of those developments within the people of God. The proof is definitely in the pudding as we must constantly be open to the possibility that the practice may come to distort the kind of people we are meant to be as the first fruits of the kingdom.

For example, we may have been wrong to discount the arguments against usury, especially as usury was first condemned as a sin against charity. A people who are pledged to care for one another so that everything they have is at the disposal of others surely must look with some concern at the attempt to make a profit from others' needs. Of course, it can be objected that borrowing is not all just for need, but to reinvest for profit and that should not be condemned. This is exactly the kind of discrimination that the casuistry of the Christian people must develop. But even if such a distinction is developed, it, of course by no means grants a blank check on all lending-for-profit practices. For example, it would seem that just as Christians would be prohibited from exploiting others within the church who are in need, so we would be prohibited from using those in need who are not in the church.

It is not my purpose, by offering these examples, to say what the church's position should be on second marriages or every form of lending, but merely to designate the process through which such matters should be determined. The church is the pioneer in displaying the implications of God's kingdom of peace brought in Jesus Christ. She does so by a relentless questioning of every aspect of her life as we learn slowly what it means to be a people of peace in every aspect of our existence. The "prohibitions" that become part of that community's life must not become minimalistic rules. Rather they should charge the imagination of the community and individuals to

But Niebuhr notes that there is yet another way of doing nothing that appears highly impracticable because it rests on the almost obsolete presupposition that there is a God. And oddly enough this view shares most with the communist assumptions about their inactivity. Like the communist, those who share such a belief do not believe simply because people can do nothing constructive that nothing constructive is being done. Like the communist, they believe that there is a force in our history that will ultimately create a different kind of world than we experience. Thus the inactivity of Christians shares with communism "the belief in the inevitably good outcome of the mundane process and the realistic insight that the good cannot be achieved by the slow accretion of better habits alone but more in consequence of a revolutionary change which will involve considerable destruction. While it does nothing it knows that something is being done, something which is divine both in its threat and its promise."[5]

Christian inactivity is such only in terms of assumptions about the efficacy of direct interference. Christians, like communists, believe something very constructive can be done in preparation for the future. Namely, Christians

> can build cells of those within each nation who, divorcing themselves from the program of nationalism and of capitalism, unite in a higher loyalty which transcends national and class lines of division and prepare for the future. There is no such Christian international today because radical Christianity has not arrived as yet at a program and a philosophy of history, but such little cells are forming. The First Christian international of Rome has had its day; the Second Christian international of Geneva or Stockholm is likely to go the way of the Second Socialist international. There is need of and opportunity for a Third Christian international.[6]

Yet Niebuhr also notes that there are great dissimilarities between Christian and communist inactivity. For the Christians, awareness of their inactivity is but a reminder of our faults, which are actually so like those of the aggressor. The American Christian must recognize that Japan is doing no more than following the example of our own country. America is no less disinterested than Japan and thus her righteous indignation is far from being righteous. So the inactivity of Christians becomes the way of repentance. The inactivity of radical Christianity, therefore, is the inaction of those who do not judge their neighbors because they cannot fool themselves into a sense of superior righteousness. It is not the inactivity of a resigned patience, but of a patience that is full of hope, and is based on faith. It is not the inactivity of the non-combatants, for it knows that there are no non-combatants, that every one is involved, that China is being crucified (though the term is very inaccurate) by our sins and those of the whole world. It is not the inactivity of the merciless, for works of mercy must be performed though they are only palliatives to ease present pain while the process of healing depends on deeper, more actual and urgent forces. But if there is no God, for if God is up in heaven and not in time itself, it is a very foolish inactivity.[7]

Thus the grace to do nothing as a Christian turns out to entail nothing less, for H. Richard Niebuhr, than a very particular faith in a definite kind of God. The patience to sustain such inactivity is possible only if the world is in fact bounded and storied by a God who has the power to use our faithfulness and unfaithfulness that the kingdom of peace might be present among us. The kind of peaceableness required of Christians is inherently tied to their acquiring the habits of peace — that is, that they are formed by a definite kind of spirituality.

The ideal of spirituality in this context is a bit odd. From a Protestant point of view the very idea of spirituality is a foreign notion because it seems to denote pious behavior that has little to do with, or is positively distracting from, the important issue of the moral life. For the Catholic, spirituality is usually associated with those "spiritual disciplines," such as prayer, meditation, and self-denial, that have no immediate connection with issues of peace or justice. Yet Niebuhr's discussion of what is required for the Christian to "do nothing" in the face of the violent alternatives of our world is in fact a counsel for the development of a spirituality necessary to sustain the commitment to peaceableness. The patience needed to remain hopeful in the face of violence requires a spiritual discipline that is grounded, as all spiritual disciplines are, in the expectation that by being so formed we will be in a position to better hear God's word for our particular lives.

The unavoidability of some account of spirituality for the Christian life is well illustrated by attending to Reinhold Niebuhr's response to his brother's position in the next issue of the *Century*. For Reinhold's position also involved a form of spirituality, but one based on quite different presuppositions than the kind of patience recommended by H. Richard. The hope that sustains such patience, according to Reinhold, is at best illusory, if not positively distorting. Reinhold does not accuse his brother of the naive hope that ethical goals such as peace can be achieved in and between societies without coercion. He recognizes that H. Richard has a "realistic interpretation of the facts of history" that acknowledges that his "moral perfectionism" is not a realistic social theory and thus must be relegated entirely to an eschatological realm. Reinhold, thus, characterizes his brother's account of Christian inactivity as the attempt to "achieve humility and disinterestedness not because enough Christians will be able by doing so to change the course of history, but because that kind of spiritual attitude is a prayer to God for the coming of his kingdom."[8]

Reinhold refuses to quarrel with this apocalyptic view as such, for he also believes that a proper eschatology is necessary to a vigorous ethic. But "what makes my brother's particular kind of eschatology impossible for me is that he identifies everything that is occurring in history (the drift toward disaster, another world war and possibly a world revolution) with the counsels of God, and then suddenly, by a leap of faith, comes to the conclusion that the same God, who uses brutalities and forces, against which man may maintain conscientious scruples, will finally establish an ideal society in which pure love will reign."[9]

Reinhold Niebuhr confesses that he finds such a faith incoherent. For how can a people's anger and resentment be said to be an instrument of God and yet at the same time an instrument they are forbidden to use in a politically effective manner because it is alleged that there are religious scruples against such a use? In contrast Reinhold argues that it would be better to use the forces of nature and history ethically to direct coercion in order that violence may be avoided, for so long as man remains man it is impossible to envisage the society of pure love that his brother seems to presuppose and for which he hopes. Man's "natural limits of reason and imagination will prevent him, even should he achieve a purely disinterested motive, from fully envisaging the needs of his fellow men or from determining his actions upon the basis of their interests. Inevitably these limitations of individuals will achieve cumulative effect in the life and actions of national, racial, and economic groups."[10]

Pure disinterestedness is thus an ideal which an individual cannot achieve and is absolutely impossible for human groups. No nation can ever be good enough to save another nation through the power of love. The best we can hope for in relations between nations is justice which seeks not perfect harmony or peace, but the adjustment of right against right, interest against interest, until some tolerable balance of power is achieved. Thus any hope of achieving a more nearly just society without the use of coercion is pure illusion. In practice this means we "must try to dissuade Japan from her military venture, but must use coercion to frustrate her designs if necessary, must reduce coercion to a minimum and prevent it from issuing in violence, must engage in constant self-analysis in order to reduce the moral conceit of Japan's critics and judges to a minimum, and must try in every social situation to maximise the ethical forces and yet not sacrifice the possibility of achieving an ethical goal because we are afraid to use any but purely ethical means."[11]

Reinhold Niebuhr says he is quite prepared to admit that his brother's "ethical perfectionism and its apocalyptic note" is closer to the gospel than his. But such an admission simply notes the inability to construct an adequate social ethic out of a pure love ethic. At the same time neither can such an ideal be abandoned, even though anything we are able to accomplish will necessarily fall short of it as an ideal. Rather the ideal must be retained for any adequate social ethic lest that ethic be lost in the relativities of expediency. "But as long as the world of man remains a place where nature and God, the real and the ideal, meet, human progress will depend upon the judicious use of the forces of nature in the service of the ideal."[12]

Confronted with Reinhold Niebuhr's realism it is easy to miss how his position also entails a very definite kind of spirituality. Moreover, it is a spirituality that demands patience and hope to sustain the Christian in the quest for the relative justice possible in this life.[13] But this kind of patience and hope is not the same as that of H. Richard Niebuhr, as Reinhold's is a patience that must confess that the history of mankind is a perennial tragedy:

> the highest ideals which the individual may project are ideals which he can never realize in social and collective terms. Love may qualify the social struggle of history but it will never abolish it, and those who make the attempt to bring society under the dominion of perfect love will die on the cross. And those who behold the cross are quite right in seeing it as a revelation of the divine, of what man ought to be and cannot be, at least not so long as he is enmeshed in the processes of history.[14]

Reinhold Niebuhr's sense of the tragic character of our existence in fact is an attempt to help train us to have souls able to keep up the struggle for justice through the inevitable and ambiguous means of coercion. Hope is surely required to sustain that endeavor, but it is not a hope, according to Niebuhr, that can seek its fulfillment within history. Rather it is a hope which realizes that its fulfillment rests beyond history, but which provides us with the means to persevere in our attempts to make our historical existence more nearly just and less violent. Yet we must never forget that those are incompatible ideals, for attempts to achieve relative justice entail at least a threat (if not explicit use) of violence. Thus, no less than the pacifist, those who would use violence for securing justice are subject to an extraordinary spiritual discipline, for they must never lose sight of the fact that they are employing a lesser evil in the hopes of achieving a relative good.

Though the question of how the United States should respond to Japan's invasion of Manchuria no longer interests us even as a theoretical question, the issues debated by the Niebuhrs in this exchange remain remarkably relevant. For example, if we substitute the issue of nuclear disarmament for the Japanese invasion, the same set of issues quickly arises. As H. Richard Niebuhr noted, we can pass resolutions, write our congressmen, but the frustrating thing is that there seems nothing constructive we can do. And the question becomes what are we to make of our lack of constructive activity and what kind of people must we be not to let our inactivity corrupt us into accepting the world and its violence as normal. Or, from the perspective of Reinhold Niebuhr, the question is what are we to make of the inevitability and necessity of some kind of nuclear standoff and what kind of people must we be not to let our possession and potential use of such weapons pervert us.[15]

Perhaps even more pressing is the question of how, if at all, we can resolve the issue as presented by the brothers Niebuhr. Both positions are well argued, both can rightly claim to represent important aspects of the Christian tradition, both certainly seem to correspond to some of our more profound intuitions. Do we simply choose one rather than the other according to what strikes us as more nearly right or confirms our unexamined intuitions? From the argument of this book obviously I think H. Richard Niebuhr's position is the one we Christians must take if we are to live in a manner appropriate to God's kingdom that has been made present in the life of Jesus of Nazareth. Yet to see the issue as choosing H. Richard Niebuhr's position rather than his brother's is a far too simple account of the matter. For I do not think the kind of position represented by H. Richard can be sustained without a spirituality very much like that hinted at by Reinhold.

2. TRAGEDY AND PEACEABLENESS

The peace Christians embody and seek is not some impossible ideal, as Reinhold Niebuhr would have it. It is not perfect harmony. It is not order that is free from conflict because it has repressed all rightful demands for justice. Rather the peaceable kingdom is a present reality, for the God who makes such a peace possible is not some past sovereign but the present Lord of the universe. Such a peace is thus just the opposite of order, as its institutionalization necessarily creates disorder and even threatens anarchy. In effect the peace of God, rather than making the world more safe, only increases the dangers we have to negotiate.

All social orders and institutions to a greater and lesser extent are built on the lie that we, not God, are the masters of our existence. In effect we enter into conspiracies of illusion to secure order because we rightly fear the anarchy and violence of disorder. We desire normalcy and safety even if that normalcy and safety is achieved at the expense of others. That is why there can finally be no separation of justice from truthfulness, for often demands for the former are challenges to our assumptions about the "way things are."

The relation between our penchant for self-deception and order can perhaps be seen more clearly at an interpersonal level than in terms of society-wide structures. Nowhere do we deceive ourselves and another more readily than in matters of love and intimacy. As creatures who are seldom sure of who we are or what we want, at least we know that we desire others to love and value us. We cannot live without esteem and we will have it even if we have to manipulate another to bestow it on us. That is, we "use" even our love and those whom we love.

But just to the extent that we do so, we commit the other, and ironically ourselves, to the living out of our deceptions. We have acquired the love and regard of another and we want to be faithful to that love. Indeed that very love seems only to reinforce our assumption that our illusions of ourselves are in fact the truth. For the very fact that another has accepted them as significant for his or her life seems to confirm their reality. Thus our deepest moral commitments work to mire us more deeply in our deceptions, as we must work all the harder to "make them true" in order to be faithful to those who love and care for us.

Those who try to protect themselves and others from such deception through frank avowals of self-interest or cynicism make particularly interesting examples of this vicious circularity. By claiming to

possess no virtue other than an unqualified pursuit of their own interests, they try to create an island of truthfulness in a sea of mendacity.
But such a strategy is doomed to failure, for cynics ironically do care;
indeed they care too much and their caring results in a self-denial
that comes close to the destruction of the self. Distrusting all, they
must finally learn to distrust even the honor and integrity of their
distrust and, thus, they are left literally worthless.

The more successful we are at our deceptions — and the very fact
that our deceptions always possess some truth means that we may be
very successful in living them out — the more we feel the necessity to
protect ourselves from any possible challenge. As a result we expand
the circle of our friends very carefully because we intuitively know
that we must not welcome any into our lives who might raise questions that challenge our illusions. Our "circle of friends" in fact
becomes a conspiracy of intimacy to protect each of our illusions, particularly insofar as those illusions are the basis of what "peace" we
know.

We thus fear the stranger who comes into our life uninitiated or
unacquainted with "our way of thinking and doing things." Often the
stranger, who may appear as our own child, insufficiently schooled
in our customs, asks a question for which there is no answer from the
perspective of our world. We learn to handle such situations through
ridicule or intolerance, thus signaling to the outsider the necessity of
accepting our way or facing continued loneliness. And more often
than not strangers "come around" to our way of seeing things, learning to forget their first awkward questions or only remembering them
as a sign of their ignorance or naivete.

Yet the stranger may persist with questions. "Why do we believe
having children is a 'good thing'?" "What is wrong with taking one's
own life?" "What is wrong with killing deformed children?" "Why
assume that one can be married to only one person at a time?" "Why
is it right to kill animals for food?" "Why should those who have in-
herited property from the past be better off than those who have
not?" "Why do we assume that God is one?" And so on. We may,
of course, try to answer such questions, for surely to each we have
some response. But we are haunted by the sense that we cannot provide, either for the stranger or ourselves, a fully adequate and per-
suasive answer. And our only recourse is to remove the presence of
the stranger and his or her questions.

In our more intimate relations the same process works, only in
a less intellectual manner. Thus the test of the honesty of any relationship between two people is often the willingness of each to allow

the other to begin a friendship with a third party that is not destined to be an equal friendship for both. For our friendships change us in ways we seldom anticipate, and when one or the other of us changes, our original relation changes. And we fear such change and find it hard not to be jealous and envious of our friend's new friend, for we feel plundered by the stranger's very presence. Knowing how difficult the achievement of any intimacy and mutual sharing is, we live in fear that the intimacy we have achieved will be destroyed by the changes brought by another. We thus increasingly live in a manner that can protect us (and hopefully those who are tied to us) from the stranger. What is, is always preferable to what might be — especially when the latter threatens change.

So we love order, even order that is based on illusion and self-deception. When we say we want peace, we mean we want order. Our greatest illusion and deception, therefore, is that we are a peaceable people, nonviolent to the core. We are peaceable so long as no one disturbs our illusions. We are nonviolent as long as no one challenges our turf. So violence becomes needlessly woven into our lives; it becomes the warp on which the fabric of our existence is threaded. The order of our lives is built on our potential for violence.[16] What is true at the personal level is even more the case when we confront one another as "societies" organized to protect and enhance our most cherished pretensions.

Thus the peace Christians desire, pray for, and receive cannot help but create instability in a world based on the assumption that violence is our ultimate weapon against disorder. Such a peace may often appear "to do nothing" exactly because it so radically challenges the presuppositions of our social order. For it is a peace that is based on the truth that requires we be hospitable to the ultimate stranger of our existence: God. God is such a stranger to us because we have chosen to live as if we were our own masters. God thus comes challenging our fears of the other by forcing us to patiently wait while others tell us their story.

There is no cure for deceptions and illusions concerning our own strength. We cannot will our way out of our fantasies, since one of our greatest fantasies is precisely that we are capable of such a will. Our only hope is the presence of the other, through which God makes present the kingdom in which we are invited to find our lives. Only in that way are we able to acquire a self, a story, that is based on trust rather than fear, peace and not violence.

Yet such a life cannot be sustained apart from a community that has so been formed by God that our constant tendency to self-deception and violence can constantly be checked. For growth in peaceableness requires, as Reinhold Niebuhr suggests, a community capable of absorbing the necessary tragedies that result without making others pay for those tragedies. But Reinhold Niebuhr was mistaken in suggesting that the tragedy which marks our existence follows from realizing that the limited good we can achieve can only be accomplished ultimately through coercion and violence. Rather that tragedy resides in the fact that the peace to which we Christians witness may well make the world more dangerous, since we do not give up our violent illusions without a struggle.[17]

Thus Christians must acquire a spirituality which will make them capable of being faithful in the face of the inexorable tragedies their convictions entail. A spirituality that acknowledges the tragic is one that is schooled in patience. As H. Richard Niebuhr suggested, our unwillingness to employ violence in order to make the world "better" means that we must often learn to wait. Yet such a waiting must resist the temptation to cynicism, conservatism, or false utopianism that assumes that the process of history will result in "everything coming out all right." For Christians hope not in "the processes of history," but in the God whom we believe has already determined the end of history in the cross and resurrection of Jesus Christ. Without such a declaration, patience in the face of the tragic could as easily be but a stoic acquiescence to fate.

The Christian commitment to living peaceably cannot be that of stoic acceptance, since the peace that has come challenges those orders, both personal and social, which promise security at the price of truth. That is why there is an inexorable connection between the peace of God and the necessity of facing the tragic character of our existence. For such a peace necessarily unsettles our compromises with violence and thus risks unleasing those forces kept in check by our conspiracies of lies. Yet the church, as the foretaste of God's kingdom, cannot fail to challenge those conspiracies and risk the hurt that may well result. There can be no justification for such a challenge except that the peace to which we witness is the truth that moves the sun and stars.

Yet there is another requirement such a peace places on us. For if it is an unsettling peace, it is also a caring peace. If Christians are required to speak the truth about our world, to challenge the powers that offer us some order, they must also be a people capable of caring for the injured that result from such a challenge. We are not a people who cause turmoil and then stand by as if we bear no responsibility for the results. No, if we are a people capable of speaking the truth, we are such only because we are also a people who refuse to abandon those whose lives have been disrupted by that truth.

Perhaps that is why the church is so often constituted by those who have at some point lost control of their lives, who have faced the darkness of rejection and anarchy. For such a people know that there is no avoiding the tragedies that are part and parcel of our histories. We cannot deny our past, but what can happen is that our past is taken up and given a new meaning through our acceptance and care of others who have faced the truth of existence. The church is thus those whose lives have been opened by God, often an opening that has extracted a great cost, and so are capable of being open to others without fear and resentment. Hospitality is part of their holiness, as they have learned to welcome the stranger as the very presence of God.

3. JOY AND PEACEABLENESS

Yet the Christian sense of tragedy that accompanies our commitment to God's peace is not the last word about the world. For if the peace we believe God has made present is unsettling it is equally the basis for joy and thanksgiving. We discover that the patient hope that requires us to wait in the face of violence is not some means to a greater good, but the good itself. Such a patience is less something we do or accomplish than it is our recognition of what God has made possible in our lives. Thus it is bad faith for Christians to let their patience be turned into resignation in the face of violence, for we know that we are not by nature violent people.

As Reinhold Niebuhr reminds us,

Christianity stands beyond tragedy. If there are tears for this man on the cross they cannot be tears of "pity and terror." The cross does not reveal life at cross purposes with itself. On the contrary, it declares that what seems to be an inherent defect in life itself is really a contingent defect in the soul of each man, the defect of the sin which he commits in his freedom. If he can realise that fact, if he can weep for himself, if he can repent, he can also be saved. He can be saved by hope and faith. His hope and faith will separate the character of life in its essential reality from life as it is revealed in sinful history.

This man on the cross who can say "Weep not for me" is also able to save us from our tears of self-pity. What he reveals about life transmutes tears of self-pity into tears of remorse and repentance. Repentance does not accuse life or God but accuses self. In that self-accusation lies the beginning of hope and salvation. If the defect lies in us and not in the character of life, life is not hopeless.[18]

Through repentance we thus learn to accept that our lives personally and socially were not meant to be tragic but joyful. And our joy is not that for which we hope, but is a present disposition that pervades our whole life. It is the presupposition of all the virtues. It is the discovery that we are not by nature liars and violent, but rightfully we are those who desire to know the truth and to live at peace with ourselves, our neighbors, and most of all God. Joy thus becomes the disposition born of a hope based on our sense that it cannot be our task to transform the violence of this world into God's peace, for in fact that has been done through the cross and resurrection of Jesus. Our joy is the simple willingness to live with the assurance of God's redemption.

It may seem strange to stress the significance of joy for the Christian life, since we normally associate joy with the momentary response to the unexpected. Joy, we think, is spontaneous but has little staying power. It cannot sustain us over the long haul. But the joy we receive as Christians is not that of a passing occasion. Rather it is a joy that derives from finding our true home among a people who carry the words and skills of God's kingdom of peace. That such a people are joyful does not mean they think that their struggle is over, for their sense of the tragic character of our existence cannot allow any shallow optimism or sentimentality. Rather their joy is possible because of their assurance that they are at least in the right struggle.

Or again it might be thought that what I am trying to talk about is happiness rather than joy. But happiness is too shallow a notion to characterize the disposition of the Christian, it too often suggests merely the satisfaction of desires determined by our selves. To be sure there are more and less profound senses of happiness, depending on the nature of our desires. But happiness, even in its most profound sense of satisfaction of a life well lived, lacks the sense of joy.[19] The joy that characterizes the Christian life is not so much the fulfillment of any desire, but the discovery that we are capable of being people who not only desire peace but are peaceable. Joy thus comes to us as a gift that ironically provides us with the confidence in ourselves which makes possible our living of God's peace as a present reality.

That is why we cannot try to be joyful even though we can try to be happy. Joy always comes to us in a form we hardly expected.

Often joy is the result of our facing what we otherwise wished to avoid and discovering that our willingness to confront the difficult or the unpleasant helped us discover that we possessed resources we did not suspect. For joy is the result of our letting go of the slim reed of security that we think provides us with the power to control our own and others' lives. But such a letting go is not something we can will, so much as it is learning to accept the whittling down that the difficulties and tragedies consequent upon our frantic search for power force on us.

Joy is thus finally a result of our being dispossessed of the illusion of security and power that is the breeding ground of our violence. Violence is not something that we "get over" through one decision to be nonviolent. Those long committed to the way of nonviolence testify to the continuing presence of violence in their lives, not the least of which is the temptation of the nonviolent to use their "weakness" to manipulate others to achieve their own ends—ends that others would pursue in a more aggressive manner. Self-deception is no less a problem of the nonviolent than the violent.

Rather nonviolence requires life-long training in being dispossessed of all that I think secures my significance and safety. And the irony is that the more we lose, the greater the possibility we have for living life joyfully. For joy is the disposition that comes from our readiness always to be surprised; or put even more strongly, joy is the disposition that comes from our realization that we can trust in surprises for the sustaining of our lives. Perhaps the most remarkable aspect of learning to live joyfully is that we learn to see the simple and most common aspects of our existence, such as our friends, our spouses, our children, as sheer gifts to which we have no right but who are nonetheless present to us.

Thus just as surely as peaceableness is a training to be patient in the face of the tragic, it is also learning to live joyfully in the face of the tragic. For the Christian hope requires that we live "beyond tragedy" insofar as we do "not regard evil as inherent in existence itself but as finally under the dominion of a good God."[20] Such a hope provides us with no basis for a sentimental optimism. It may well be that we must learn to "do nothing," at least in the sense of action that will have clear, constructive results, in the face of this nation's invasion of that nation, or in terms of our policy of "mutually assured destruction" for the control of nuclear weapons. Yet we can be a people who witness confidently to the peace that we know is possible in this life, since we have begun to feel its power in our lives. For what hope has the world if there are not "cells" of people who manifest a joy that otherwise the world would have no means of knowing to be possible in this life?

4. ON THE GRACE OF DOING ONE THING

It may seem odd to end a book designed to introduce the student to Christian ethics with a discussion of "spirituality" and in particular tragedy and joy. Yet every ethic, whether it does so explicitly or not, involves recommendations about the means by which our lives should come to embody what is said to be the good and the true. To avoid the issue of spirituality is to risk an abstractness that belies the seriousness of our claims. Any proposal about the Christian life is not just a group of ideas about how we might live, but a claim about how we should live if we are to be faithful to the God of Israel and Jesus.[21]

Moreover, the position taken in this book, as I suggested earlier, is almost self-defeating, since most of us feel completely unprepared to live in a nonviolent manner. Even if we are convinced that Christian convictions entail such a life, we despair at our ability to make that life actual. My discussion of the sense of tragedy that accompanies such a life as well as the joy that results has been meant to provide the imaginative holds necessary for us at least to envision what it would mean for us to live peaceably. For the Christian life is more a recognition and training of our senses and passions than a matter of choices and decisions. By displaying some of the sense and passion of that life, we may all be better able to see how to live it.

But I am still acutely aware that such a way of life does not come easily. None of us knows the depth of our violence. As I have tried to suggest, the very idea of renouncing all possibilities of violence from our lives frightens us, for it seems to entail the surrender of all control over our lives—indeed it seems to suggest that we give up the very thing that allows us to have a self at all.

Perhaps that is just the clue we need to know where we can start, for we have been schooled to think that if we are to be moral we must find ways to deal with the "problems of the world." We must, thus, find ways to deal with world hunger; we must discover how to institutionalize more fully world justice; we must find a way of extending to all people the "freedom" we enjoy in America. But confronted with such mammoth challenges we feel that we can do nothing. Where is one to start? By acquiring power at the top? And we discover, even if we do start there, such power is not sufficient, since any steps to alleviate world hunger must be balanced against other foreign policy objectives designed to keep the world in order.

No, we must remember that the violence that provides the resources for the powers of the world to do their work lies in each of our souls. That does not mean that we can begin only by changing hearts and then, later, look to wider structural issues. Indeed that is a false dichotomy, since our hearts are also within the wider structures. Rather it means that I do not have to think about doing everything or nothing; I do not have to begin by trying to "solve" the real problem. Instead I can take the time to do one thing that might help lead myself and others to God's peace.

As David Burrell points out,

> unless we take the sort of steps which are on a scale modest enough to be incorporated into our own story, we may easily fail to see how the gospel can "apply." If we do begin to alter the pattern of our lives, however, we will have to explain those actions to ourselves and those close to us. And, as those explanations become part of the fabric of our story, we will be helped to see how the stories of the scriptures help to shape ours as well. What differentiates a constructive response from an ideological reaction is that the first, by definition, alters the patterns of our own lives, while the second rails against "them."[22]

By not trying to do everything, but to do one thing that applies to ourselves and alters our lives, we are led further into God's peaceable kingdom. For that "one thing" is just enough to remove us from the familiar world of violence so that our imagination might be freed to find yet one other thing we might do. For example, by being a member of a church we might find that we are tied to other churches in other lands in a more profound manner than we are tied to our nation. "Travel" becomes possible or required, since we now realize that we are not tied to place but to a people who are always on the move.

It may be objected that the saints and the models of ascetic practice often did not ever travel and they seemed none the worse for it. But that is just the point, because ascetic disciplines are the means to learn to travel in one place. For example, learning the discipline to wait, to be at rest with ourselves, to take the time to be a friend and to be loved, are all ascetic practices that are meant to free us from the normalcy of the world. Through them we are slowly recalled from the world of violence that we might envisage how interesting a people at peace might be.

Perhaps the thing that most holds us to the world of violence is our fear that the alternative would entail constant boredom. We need and thrive on conflict, which we assume entails violence. To be lured into the world of nonviolence requires a transformation of our imaginations. We must come to see how exciting an adventure is entailed by God's offer of peace. But even more than seeing, we come to experience that peace in ourselves and with our friends here and now because we have the assurance that God has made his peace a present reality through his spirit. We can thus take the time to build, as H. Richard Niebuhr suggests, those cells within each nation that unite in a higher loyalty than nation or class—that are in fact God's international.

It may be objected that in a world poised on the brink of nuclear annihilation this is not enough. We must do more. But again as Burrell reminds us,

> we are never enjoined [in the Scriptures] to *accomplish* anything. The recurring theme of the psalmist, who summarizes as only poets can the sweep of God's covenanting with his people, is that we are to recount—often and loudly—God's *accomplishments*, his great deeds on our behalf. And we? We are asked to be faithful—as he is faithful. Faithful to the way as it will be shown to us by those he sends, his prophets. And, Jesus expresses it similarly when, speaking to his disciples in John's farewell discourse, he reminds them that they did not choose him: "no, I chose you; and I commissioned you to go out and to bear fruit, fruit that will last" (John 15:16). . . . But, it also spells out the meaning of the startling statement immediately preceding: "I shall not call you servants any more, . . . I call you friends" (John 15:15).
>
> As his friends we are liberated from having to prove ourselves by accomplishing great deeds. We are already accepted as intimates. Yet, we are not dispensed from the response characteristic of friendship: to become what the other's trust would call forth from us. Bearing fruit is more like becoming something than doing something; yet, the results are not only tangible, they are nourishing for others. Bearing fruit is to let ourselves become gift for others. As he did, as he is.[23]

Such is the grace of doing one thing. But it is the one thing that draws on the very truth of our existence and the power that sustains the vast depths of the universe. We do it, not because it is effective, but simply because it is true.

Postscript

Twenty Years Later

I wish I could remember writing this book. Surely an author ought to be able to remember writing a book even if it has been twenty years since the book was written. However, I do not remember if I wrote the book during the school year when I was teaching the course in Christian Ethics for Notre Dame undergraduates, or if I wrote it the summer before or the summer after I had finished teaching the course. I may have written it before, after, or during. I would like to remember writing the book, because I discovered rereading the book to write this "Postscript" that I still think this is not only a good book but one that, after twenty years, is worth reading.

I am, therefore, grateful that SCM Press has decided to make *The Peaceable Kingdom: A Primer in Christian Ethics* available to a new generation of readers. The book has never gone out of print in America and still sells well, year in and year out. I hope that is because many teachers still find the challenge to conventional ethics courses the book represents not only useful but important for how ethics is taught. Dr. James Langford, the director of Notre Dame Press, who (as I report in the "Preface" of the 1983 edition suggested I write a book like *The Peaceable Kingdom*) had quite a different account of a book's longevity. Jim praised the "yellow notes" from which professors taught the same course the same way year after year. From Jim's perspective, their unwillingness to do anything new sold books. I do not think he had *The Peaceable Kingdom* explicitly in mind when he expounded this theory, but I suspect he thought in the long run the theory might apply.

I hope he is wrong, however, about the staying power of *The Peaceable Kingdom*. At the very least the very character of the book makes it doubtful that those that use the book in ethics courses do so out of lethargy. *The Peaceable Kingdom* was written to make the brains of those reading the book hurt. I did not write the book to be just "another alternative" that might be taken into account alongside other ethical theories. Rather I wrote the book to change lives, that is, to develop the conceptual tools necessary to help Christians recover the extraordinary imaginary entailed by God's invitation to be members in the body and blood of Christ.

At least one of the challenges *The Peaceable Kingdom* presented to teacher and student alike was whether it was really a book in "ethics." In Catholic circles the book did not seem to be about ethics, because it did not begin with considerations of natural law.[1] In Protestant circles the "ethics" of *The Peaceable Kingdom* also seemed far too "theological." From the Protestant point of view, it was thought best to keep Christian ethics as free as possible of explicit theological claims because theological affirmations made it more difficult to be a "player" in a "pluralist" society. Yet by the time I was writing *The Peaceable Kingdom*, I had realized I was not an ethicist who used theology but rather I was a theologian. Indeed I hoped that *The Peaceable Kingdom* might be used in theology courses as well as courses in ethics. For if I was critical of ethicists for not recognizing the theological center of ethics, I thought theologians remiss for their failure to recognize the practical character of theological convictions.

I had written four books prior to *The Peaceable Kingdom*.[2] Some might suggest the claim "I had written four books" prior to *The Peaceable Kingdom* to be misleading. *Character and the Christian Life* is the only book prior to *The Peaceable Kingdom* that might count as a book. The other "books" were collections of essays I put together to make them look like books. I have no reason to resist those who would so describe the way I have put my books together and continue to put my books together. The essay continues to be the way I prefer to write because I understand my work, as the sub-title of *Truthfulness and Tragedy* suggests, to be "Further Investigations in Christian Ethics." The operative word is "investigations."

However, *The Peaceable Kingdom* is a book. It is not a collection of essays, but rather a book whose chapters were written in the sequential order in which they appear in the book. I do not want to leave the impression that *The Peaceable Kingdom* is a book in contrast to my books of essays because the order of the chapters "makes more sense." I try to think hard about how my books of essays are to be put together. Indeed I often write an essay in relation to the essays I have already written with the intended book in mind. By suggesting that *The Peaceable Kingdom* is a book in contrast to my other books, I mean only to indicate that the writing and form of *The Peaceable Kingdom* conforms to the standard most people associate with a "book."

Yet I do not deny that *The Peaceable Kingdom*, given the work I had published in my earlier books, appeared to be different. *The Peaceable Kingdom* is less polemical than my earlier or subsequent books of essays. Indeed one of my worries about the book is that it could be read too piously. In *The Peaceable Kingdom* I risk using first order Christian language about what it means to be a disciple of Christ. I have no problem with the language, but I fear using the language means some reading the book may think I am recommending that we need something like "a personal relationship with Jesus." Pious sentimentalities are often harmless, but I fear such sentiments can prevent Christian speech from doing any useful work because they foster internally referential enclaves that have no purchase on how the world is.

By the time I wrote *The Peaceable Kingdom*, however, I was increasingly aware that I could not write *about* theology and ethics. I had to do theology. That may sound very odd to those that are not theologians, but it is not at all strange in the current academic world of theology, for theologians to assume a position "outside" that about which they write. Indeed as Alasdair MacIntyre once observed, Roman Catholic moral theologians no longer seem interested in God: rather, they are passionately interested in other Roman Catholic moral theologians. That judgement unfortunately describes a great deal of the work done in theology.

The Peaceable Kingdom was my attempt to write in a manner that God matters. I hope that my previous work was not devoid of that ambition. I certainly could not have written *The Peaceable Kingdom* if I had not written the previous books. They represented the necessary exercises I needed to acquire not only the skills but also the confidence to write a book like *The Peaceable Kingdom*. I was still a relatively young man when I wrote this book. Nothing is quite as silly, moreover, than someone trying at an early age to be more wise than they are – which is one of the reasons I wish I could remember writing the book. I wonder how to account for the person that wrote the book because I am surprised that I was enough of a Christian to write it.

The truth of the matter is that I doubt my own subjectivity at the time was up to the task. What made the book possible was the extraordinary community that surrounded me, a Protestant, at the University of Notre Dame. There are certainly individuals, as I hope the footnotes of *The Peaceable Kingdom* indicate, such as David Burrell and John Howard Yoder, that made me more than I otherwise could be. But just as important were the many Masses I attended at Sacred Heart Church on the campus of Notre Dame, as well as the expectations of the students I was teaching.

That is why I think it is important for understanding *The Peaceable Kingdom* to have some sense of the context that was the University of Notre Dame. Most of the students that took the course in Christian Ethics were Roman Catholics, but that does not mean they knew much about what it meant for them to be Roman Catholics. But most of the students had come through parochial Catholic schools, which meant they thought Christianity mattered, even if for some of them it mattered that they rejected what seemed to them the authoritarian character of Catholicism. What an extraordinary resource for someone like me. I did not have to write *The Peaceable Kingdom* for those that might consider Christianity if someone could make the Christian faith an attractive alternative for their "life style." Rather I could teach and write Christian Ethics for students who were just Christian enough that they might be ready to be surprised about how extraordinary this "Christian stuff" is and could be.

In truth, until I reread *The Peaceable Kingdom* in preparation for this "Postscript," I had forgotten what a "Catholic" book it is. By "Catholic" I do not mean anyone reading the book is likely to misidentify me as a Roman Catholic moral theologian. Rather, by describing the book as "Catholic" I mean to call attention to how many of my conversation partners were Roman Catholic. That I directed criticism toward Roman Catholic moral theologians such as Timothy O'Connell as well as criticized the concept of "fundamental option" no doubt betrayed my being deeply embedded in a Catholic culture. I hope, however, one of the reasons that *The Peaceable Kingdom* remains interesting involves my attempt to suggest how developments in Catholic thought indicate challenges facing all Christians.

I am often asked by people what book they should read to understand what I am about. That question is usually asked because the one asking the question has realized there is too much Hauerwas to read, but they nonetheless would like to have some sense of the way I think. I normally recommend *The Peaceable Kingdom*.[3] The book certainly does depend on and may even "pull together" the reflections I had developed in my earlier books. Yet I worry that those reading *The Peaceable Kingdom* may think by doing so they "have got" what I think needs to be said about how Christians should think about how they live, or, even more important, how we live. That *The Peaceable Kingdom* was meant as an introductory text may give the impression that the account I give in the book is in some manner comprehensive.

The Peaceable Kingdom, however, is no less investigative than my books of essays. By "investigative" I do not mean the book is tentative, if by "tentative" is meant that I was only making suggestions about how Christians might think about how we are to live as Christians. *The Peaceable Kingdom* represents what I continue to think about how Christians should live. Rather, by "investigative" I mean that the *position* (a word I do not like to use just to the extent it suggests that what I think may be more important than what the church does) I take in *The Peaceable Kingdom* is less a "summing up" than "a way to go on" that requires the continuing hard work of reflection.[4] I have written many books since I wrote *The Peaceable Kingdom*. I have done so because I must continue to force myself to think through what I have said in *The Peaceable Kingdom*. If *The Peaceable Kingdom* pulled it "all together," it seems in my subsequent work I have been trying to take it apart in order to understand how it came together.

I hope, therefore, that readers kind enough to read this postscript to the new edition of *The Peaceable Kingdom* will consider reading the book again. I have spent the last twenty years "reading" what I wrote in *The Peaceable Kingdom*, and I am still not sure I understand what was said through me in this book. That is why I still like the book. I continue to be surprised by what I had forgotten or not noticed I had written. To live "out of control" is the primary description of what it means to be a Christian in *The Peaceable Kingdom*.[5] When Christians try to control the worlds in which we find ourselves – even the worlds of our own books – too often our imaginations die. But living "out of control" is hard work. That is why it is important that *The Peaceable Kingdom* continues to unsettle the presumption, including the presumption of the author of *The Peaceable Kingdom*, that the God we worship can ever be adequately described or domesticated. Every time you finish saying what you think needs to be said, if what you have said is faithful to the God who has called us in Christ, then you must begin again.

I decided a "Postscript" was more appropriate for the new edition of *The Peaceable Kingdom* than a preface to the book with a new "Introduction." If I had tried to write an "Introduction," I did not think I could resist the temptation to tell new readers of the book what they were going to read (which is not necessarily a "bad thing" if you remember that virtue – and in particular the virtues acquired through reading – require repetition). If what I argue in *The Peaceable Kingdom* is close to being right, about the worst possible thing I could do is to try to explain what I was trying to do in the book. If I could explain what I was trying to do, then the reader would rightly worry if they needed to read the book – much less, as I just suggested, read the book again.

The Peaceable Kingdom requires rereading not only because it tries to unsettle normal presumptions about "ethics," but also because I need the continuing help of readers to understand the implications of the book. One of the ways to understand *The Peaceable Kingdom* is to think of it as a quite massive language transforming proposal. If the main outlines of the argument of *The Peaceable Kingdom* are right, then too often the very way we speak, the habits of our language, betray what we should know. For example, I often find sentences in *The Peaceable Kingdom* whose grammar betrays the argument of the book. For example, consider this sentence: "'Sanctification' is but a way of reminding us of the kind of journey we must undertake if we are to make the story of Jesus our story."[6] The verb "make" in that sentence is too strong. The sentence should have read: "'Sanctification' is but a way of reminding us of the journey we must discover God has made possible through the life, death, and resurrection of Christ." I hope those reading *The Peaceable Kingdom* will find their own sentences to rewrite.

Such an exercise is particularly important given the contention with which the book starts. The claim that all "ethics" requires a qualifier is not only a descriptive statement about any "ethic" we might encounter, but as I hope readers discover, such a claim turns out to entail a metaphysics required by the recognition that all that is is created. I do not pretend that all that needs to be said about how these two claims are connected is said in *The Peaceable Kingdom*; but I hope I said enough in this book that others intrigued by the suggestion of the interrelation of these claims will explore further what more needs to be said. I know I continue to worry these questions, for they are obviously at the heart of my book, *With the Grain of The Universe: The Church's Witness and Natural Theology* as well as *Performing the Faith: Bonhoeffer and the Practice of Nonviolence.*[7]

Hopefully therefore, *The Peaceable Kingdom*, in spite of the claim in the subtitle that it is a "Primer," is a book that can be read for profit by those beginning theological reflection as well as those who may properly be called theologians. John Howard Yoder – explaining why he has never tried to write "a basic introduction" to his thought as he suggested I did in *The Peaceable Kingdom* – observes I called the book a "primer" but the book fits none of the three things a primer can mean. Yoder notes *The Peaceable Kingdom*:

is not a primer in the elementary-education sense, a book for beginning to read in the first grade, because it does not start at the beginning simply, nor does it track a curriculum. It is not a primer, secondly, in the sense of the first coat of paint, intended to fill the pores of a wood surface, or to heighten the adhesiveness of a metal surface, so that a later coat of the real paint will stick better. Nor is it (thirdly) like the first gallon of water poured into a pump to wet the leather around the plunger and thereby augment the vacuum drawing the water up from a well. (*Webster's* has two other meanings for "primer" and they do not fit either.) *The Peaceable Kingdom* was as selective and as idiosyncratic as Hauerwas' earlier writings, even though it differed from them in having been written all in one piece. Were I to try to write a book like that, I do not know what it would be about.[8]

I wish I could claim credit for the use of the description "Primer" in the subtitle to *The Peaceable Kingdom*, but Jim Langford (then the director of the University of Notre Dame Press) suggested that the book be called a Primer. He did so because once I had written the book, it was clear that it was not an introductory text if "introductory" was meant to describe a book that reports on what others are thinking. But it was nonetheless a book that hopefully could be read by a student not far along in the study of theology and ethics. I am not sure what Langford thought the word "primer" meant. But in spite of Yoder's claim that the word inadequately describes the book, I think all three meanings he identifies do indicate something about the book. However, the third meaning is particularly helpful because if the book was meant to do anything it was to "prime the pump." That is why, moreover, the book hopefully can be beneficially read by beginners as well as the more accomplished.

Moreover, I think the book can profitably be read twenty years later. No doubt it will read differently than it read in 1983. In 1983 postmodernism was not widely recognized as a new intellectual development. Some may read the anti-foundationalism that certainly shapes *The Peaceable Kingdom* as an early harbinger of what is now called postmodernism, but I have no interest in being so classified.[9] I am much more interested in what those reading the book today make of my account of sin as a theological achievement or my contention that "revelation" is not an epistemological category. Equally interesting for me would be a discussion of my attempt to show why any adequate Christology cannot be separated from discipleship. To be sure that is a lesson I learned from John Howard Yoder, but I continue to find it odd that few seem to think that lesson as important as I do.

I am also extremely interested in what contemporary readers make of the way *The Peaceable Kingdom* is organized. The first three chapters are "introductory" because the book really starts in Chapter Four. Yet I had to find some way to develop the conceptual machinery, that is, to introduce concepts such as narrative and character in the beginning chapters of the book without them appearing to try to develop an anthropological starting point after the fashion of liberal Protestant theology. I tried to begin without the beginning betraying what was to come. At the same time I wanted the early chapters to be interesting to read. Accordingly, I decided to introduce what it means to learn to be a sinner in Chapter Two, even though I was afraid that, particularly because of my use of Reinhold Niebuhr's account of sin, I might reproduce liberal mistakes. I hoped, however, that the account of sin as self-deception in Chapter Three – and particularly how that account requires a quite different understanding of human action than Niebuhr presupposes – is sufficient to distance me from Niebuhr's general theological position.[10]

Along the same lines, I hope some might notice that I do not try to develop an account of the virtues until Chapter Six. Any attention my work first received was related to my attempt to reintroduce the virtues as important for ethics. That was appropriate because I certainly began my work trying to reclaim the significance of the virtues for understanding better the character of well-lived lives. But I began to worry that many seemed to think "virtue ethics" was an alternative to other formal ethical theories. So I deliberately introduced the virtues in the chapter on the church in order to stress that the Christian virtues depend for their specification on the concrete practices of the church. As far as I know, few have discussed my contention in *The Peaceable Kingdom* that the virtues of hope and patience are the crucial virtues if we are to rightly understand the eschatological – or perhaps better, the apocalyptic – character of the Christian faith.[11] That does not mean I think Aquinas was wrong to maintain that charity is the form of the virtues. But I do think that Aquinas's failure to develop the importance of hope, and the patience hope requires, suggests that his overall perspective is insufficiently eschatological. Of course, Aquinas never forgot we are wayfarers; but it is not clear in Aquinas if the way on which we fare is that determined by the Christian anticipation of the kingdom of God.

I fear in the last few paragraphs I have begun to do what I promised myself I would not do in this "Postscript," that is, to explain to the reader what you have just read. However, before I close I want to respond to a question I am often asked by readers of *The Peaceable*

Kingdom. They want to know who the person was on the plane that turned down the proposition of the stewardess (pp. 129–130). It was me. I did not identify myself in the book because I generally do not like appeals to "my experience." Nor did I want to call attention to my "integrity" – even the compromised integrity I hope I adequately made clear was the best I could do at the time.

However, I do care about telling the truth even when I have to recognize that it is not at all clear I know what the truth is or whether I am telling the truth for reasons other than being truthful. Yet I hope it is clear to the readers of *The Peaceable Kingdom* that the book was written to help us be truth-bearers in a world that is constituted by lies and even worse, half-truths. I am convinced that nonviolence and truth-bearing are inseparable. If the reader of *The Peaceable Kingdom* gets some hint why that may be from engaging this book, I will be more than satisfied.

Notes

1. CHRISTIAN ETHICS IN A FRAGMENTED AND VIOLENT WORLD

1. This way of putting the matter is misleading in itself, for to insist on a qualifier seems to assume the "ethics" is an identifiable activity prior to the qualifier. Yet that is certainly not the case for religious traditions. The Western philosophical tradition, however, has developed a relatively coherent account of "ethics" as the investigation and analysis of the good. However, that tradition is marked by deep disagreements that certainly defeat any attempts to make ethics an integral discipline.

2. Thus the very interesting development of courses in medical ethics, business ethics, legal ethics, professional ethics in our colleges and universities. While not a bad thing in themselves, such courses cannot pretend to supply an adequate "ethic" for the various activities, much less ensure that the practitioners will act "ethically" as the result of such courses. This is not because of a lack of good will but because the very meaning of "ethics" is an essentially contested concept.

3. For a critique of quandary ethics see Edmund Pincoff's "Quandary Ethics" in *Revisions: Changing Perspectives in Moral Philosophy*, ed. Stanley Hauerwas and Alasdair MacIntyre (Notre Dame, Ind.: University of Notre Dame Press, 1983), pp. 92–111.

4. Alasdair MacIntyre, *After Virtue* (Notre Dame, Ind.: University of Notre Dame Press, 1981), p. 1.

5. Ibid., p. 2. For a more extended analysis of MacIntyre's important book see my and Paul Wadell's review in *The Thomist* 46/2 (April 1982), pp. 313–322.

6. Peter Berger, *The Heretical Imperative* (Garden City, N.Y.: Anchor Press, 1979).

7. Ibid., p. 25. Though I find Berger's analysis provocative, I do not agree with some of his methodological presuppositions — such as the very concept of "plausibility structure."

8. MacIntyre, *After Virtue*, p. 22.

9. Ibid., p. 30.

10. Immanuel Kant, *Foundations of the Metaphysics of Morals* (New York: The Liberal Arts Press, 1959), p. 39.

11. Aristotle, *The Nichomachean Ethics*, trans. Martin Ostwald (Indianapolis: Bobbs-Merrill, 1962), 1094b15–27.

12. For a discussion of these issues see *Religion and Morality*, ed. Gene Outka and John Reeder (Garden City, N.Y.: Anchor Press, 1973).

13. John Coleman exemplifies this tension in his recent and very fine book, *An American Strategic Theology* (New York: Paulist Press, 1982). Coleman sees better than most that Catholicism's contribution to the American polity requires the maintenance of a disciplined community, but just to the extent that American Catholics become assimilated within American society the basis of that discipline is undermined.

14. I do not mean to deny the significance of faith for understanding religious belief and practice. For example, see Wilfred Smith's *Faith and Belief* (Princeton, N.J.: Princeton University Press, 1979), and David Burrell's insightful review of Smith's work, "Faith and Religious Convictions: Studies in Comparative Epistemology," *Journal of Religion* 63 (1983), 64–73. What I am objecting to is the tendency of modern theology to handle its theological program apologetically by attempting to show that faith is an unavoidable aspect of human experience such that religious convictions, whether true or not, are unavoidable.

15. For example, see *The Significance of Atheism* by Alasdair MacIntyre and Paul Ricoeur (New York: Columbia University Press, 1969).

16. As Lessing put it, "If no historical truth can be demonstrated, then nothing can be demonstrated by means of historical truths. That is: accidental truths of history can never become the proof of necessary truths of reason." And, of course, it is only the latter that we think capable of sustaining a true morality. Like Lessing, we fail to see that almost all "necessary truths of reason" are fundamentally uninteresting or illusory. "On the Proof of the Spirit and of Power," in *Lessing's Theological Writings*, translated with an Introduction by Henry Chadwick (London: Adam and Charles Black, 1956), p. 53.

2. A QUALIFIED ETHIC: THE NARRATIVE CHARACTER OF CHRISTIAN ETHICS

1. Bernard Williams, *Morality: An Introduction to Ethics* (New York: Harper & Row, 1972), pp. 29–39.

2. Ibid., p. 29.

3. Ibid., p. 11. For a similar argument see my "Learning to See Red Wheelbarrows: On Vision and Relativism," *Journal of the American Academy of Religion* 45 (June 1977), 644–655.

4. Williams, *Morality*, pp. 3–4.

5. See David Solomon, "Rules and Principles," *Encyclopedia of Bioethics*, Vol. I., ed. Warren Reich (New York: The Free Press, 1978), pp. 407–413. See also G. J. Warnock's *The Object of Morality* (New York: Methuen, 1971) for an analysis of rules and their relation to the virtues.

6. See Alasdair MacIntyre's *After Virtue* (Notre Dame, Ind.: University of Notre Dame Press, 1981), p. 12.

7. For example, William Frankena simply assumes in his widely influential *Ethics* that the question "What ought I (or we) to do?" is primary. *Ethics*, 2nd ed. (Englewood Cliffs, N.J.: Prentice-Hall, 1973), p. 12.

8. For example, see the exchange between Frankena and me in the *Journal of Religious Ethics* 3 (Spring 1975), 27–62.

9. For a more complete account of these alternatives than that given above see Frankena's *Ethics*, pp. 14–20.

10. See, for example, Paul Ramsey's stress on covenant in his book, *The Patient as Person* (New Haven: Yale University Press, 1969).

11. The classical statement of this position, for all its oversimplification, remains Joseph Fletcher's *Situation Ethics* (Philadelphia: Westminster Press, 1966). Ramsey, of course, began his work stressing love as the central, if not overriding, concept for Christian ethics. However, he was forced to employ the conceptually clumsy device of "rule inprincipled love" to distinguish his position from Fletcher's. For example, see Ramsey's *Deeds and Rules in Christian Ethics* (New York: Charles Scribner's Sons, 1967), pp. 117–144. Ramsey's development of the theme of covenant fidelity, while present from the beginning, in his later work provided a more appropriate expression for his basic insights.

12. See, for example, Anthony Phillips's treatment of the decalogue in his, *Ancient Israel's Criminal Law* (New York: Schocken Books, 1970).

13. MacIntyre, *After Virtue*, p. 135. Also see his discussion on pp. 163ff.

14. For a fuller analysis of the place of narrative in theology see Michael Goldberg's *Theology and Narrative: A Critical Introduction* (Nashville: Abingdon, 1982).

15. The creeds are often attempts to discriminate between various accounts of the story. They thus act as a critical guide to help us to know better which of the accounts are insufficient. But the creeds do not determine *the* story, as if it is a single story, but rather they mark the stories that should rightly command our attention in our attempt to be faithful to God.

16. Kenneth Schmitz, *The Gift: Creation* (Milwaukee: Marquette

University Lectures, 1982), pp. 47–48. Schmitz uses this point to suggest that the gifted character of our existence is what is at stake in the doctrine of *creation ex nihilo*.

17. Schmitz, p. 56.

18. I am indebted to Philip Foubert for helping me distinguish these.

19. For example, Paul Ricoeur insightfully argues that "No biblical narrative works merely as narrative. It receives not only its theological but even its original religious meaning from its composition with other modes of discourse. I have underlined elsewhere the unbreakable conjunction between narratives and Laws within the Torah. Laws transform narratives into instruction and narratives transform Law into gift. Then we are led to acknowledge that the Hebraic tradition is prevented from becoming a mystifying ideology, thanks to its dialectical relation to prophecy. Prophecy, on the one hand, reveals within the narratives themselves the potential of unfulfilled promises which re-orient the story of the past toward the future. Narratives, on the other hand, provide the eschatological anticipation of the 'new' era with images and types. This typological use of past stories for the sake of the projection of the future gives to the narratives themselves a meaningfulness which is quite alien to ordinary story-telling. Furthermore, we have to take into account the deep impact of the wisdom literature on the narratives themselves which henceforth display the imprint of perpetuity characteristic of the wisdom sayings. This transfiguration of narratives through wisdom, added to the typological use of past stories for the sake of the anticipation of the era to come, puts biblical narratives outside the stream of popular story-telling. Finally, the re-enactment of the narratives in the cultic situation and their recounting through the Psalms of praise, of lamentation and of penitence, complete the complex intertwining between narrative and non-narrative modes of discourse. The whole range of modes may thus be seen as distributed between the two poles of storytelling and praising. This dialectic between narrative and non-narrative expressions of the faith is neither weakened nor simplified in the New Testament writings. On the contrary, the 'new utterance' — to use Amos Wilder's phrase — generates new polarities such as the new and the old, the already there and the not yet, whose tensions give to the New Testament narratives a special style. These tensions become conspicuous when we compare the minimal narratives of the purely Kerygmatic expressions of faith and the extended narratives of the synoptic tradition. In this tradition the relation between proclamation and narrative may appear as a retrieval within the New Testament of the Old Testament polarity of praise and narration." "Toward a Narrative Theology," Address given at Haverford College, Spring 1982, pp. 16–17.

20. For an extraordinary account of the narrative character and art of the Hebrew scripture see Robert Alter, *The Art of Biblical Narrative* (New

York: Basic Books, 1981). Alter argues that there is an intrinsic connection between Israel's monotheism and the narrative art displayed in Hebrew Scripture, as the former necessarily creates the space that makes necessary the display of intentional activity. Though Alter's insistence on monotheism as the hallmark of the conception of God in Scripture is overdrawn, his essential point seems to me right.

21. Reinhold Niebuhr, *The Nature and Destiny of Man* (New York: Charles Scribner's Sons, 1957), pp. 178–179.

3. ON BEING HISTORIC: AGENCY, CHARACTER, AND SIN

1. The importance of our nature for the moral life has generally been overlooked in modern ethics because of its stress on freedom. Yet it is our nature, particularly in the form of our desires, that forces us to be moral. Lust, for example, certainly can be chaotic, but it can also set us on a way of life that makes us care about something. It is therefore a precious resource which we cannot do without.

2. Conrad's depiction of Martin Decoud in *Nostromo* is one of his most compelling portraits in this respect.

3. Frithjof Bergmann, *On Being Free* (Notre Dame, Ind.: University of Notre Dame Press, 1977), p. 57. I am indebted to Bergmann's analysis for the argument of this chapter, for reasons that should be obvious.

4. Aristotle, *Nichomachean Ethics,* trans. Martin Ostwald (Indianapolis: Bobbs-Merrill, 1962), 1114b1–7.

5. Stanley Hauerwas, *Character and the Christian Life* (San Antonio: Trinity University Press, 1975), p. 115.

6. Gene Outka, "Character, Vision, and Narrative," *Religious Studies Review* 6/2 (April 1980), p. 112.

7. Alasdair MacIntyre, *After Virtue* (Notre Dame, Ind.: University of Notre Dame Press, 1981), p. 202.

8. Timothy O'Connell, *Principles for a Catholic Morality* (New York: Seabury, 1978), p. 59.

9. Ibid., p. 60.

10. Ibid.

11. Ibid., p. 62.

12. Ibid., p. 63.

13. Ibid., p. 64.

14. Ibid., p. 65.

15. Charles Taylor's *Explanation of Behavior* (Atlantic Highlands, N.J.: Humanities, 1964) still seems to me to be one of the best defenses of these points.

and that the theologian's task is basically to see that some are not emphasized to the expense of others—thus it is said, "some Protestant theologians
deny the goodness of creation," p. 39. But the issue is what is meant by creation, or sin, and how such notions derive their intelligibility from Christian
tradition. Curran's use of these terms turns them into lifeless abstractions.

This is not to deny that "nature" is an essential category for theological
reflection. But that it is so does not mean that nature has an integrity sufficient to sustain an autonomous ethic. We are "natural" to the extent that
God has created us capable of receiving his grace. We thus are by nature—
that is, by God's will—beings independent of God. Yet our nature must remain incomplete, since by nature we are not sufficient in ourselves. Nature
as a theological concept will always be ambiguous, since it is necessary for
theological reflection, yet it cannot ever be intelligibly displayed or analyzed
in itself. This way of putting the matter I owe to Professor Nicholas Lash.

13. It is interesting to note that when creation-redemption, nature-
grace are made primary in order to underwrite a universal ethic there is a
tendency to justify violence as a legitimate form of Christian behavior. For
it is alleged that Christians must take responsibility for "creation" even if it
means the use of violence. Moreover the "redemption" wrought becomes an
ideal that is explicated in abstraction from Jesus' life and teaching. Thus
Jesus' redemption is affirmed but not in a manner that we must take his
teachings seriously for the guiding of our lives. But Jesus' "redemption" is
not in discontinuity with his teaching, for unless we take the latter seriously
we cannot know the meaning of the former.

14. Joseph Fuchs, "Is There a Specifically Christian Morality?" in
Readings in Moral Theology, No. 2: The Distinctiveness of Christian Ethics,
ed. Charles Curran and Richard McCormick (New York: Paulist Press,
1980), pp. 5–6.

15. Ibid., p. 7.

16. Ibid., p. 8.

17. Ibid., p. 15.

18. Richard McCormick, "Does Faith Add to Ethical Perception," in
Readings in Moral Theology, No. 2: The Distinctiveness of Christian Ethics,
ed. Charles Curran and Richard McCormick, p. 169.

19. For example, see my response to Richard Neuhaus's statement,
"Christianity and Democracy" in the *Center Journal* 1/3 (Summer 1982),
pp. 42–51.

20. McCormick, p. 157.

21. This is an issue largely overlooked in most Christian systematic
theology. John Howard Yoder has done more than anyone to reestablish the
significance and primacy of church-world categories. For example, see Yoder's
Christian Witness to the State (Newton, Kansas: Faith and Life Press, 1977).

22. The command to forgive our enemies should surely be the most provocative reminder of how misleading is the claim that Christian ethics is human ethics. Human ethics is built on the assumption of the legitimacy of self-defense — as are also most accounts of natural law ethics that legitimate survival as the source of moral principles. On the other hand, Christian ethics severely qualifies that "desire."

23. Alasdair MacIntyre, *After Virtue* (Notre Dame, Ind.: University of Notre Dame Press, 1981), p. 197.

24. Ibid., p. 205.

25. McCormick, p. 157.

26. Gerald Hughes, *Authority in Morals* (London: Heythrop College, 1978), pp. v–vi.

27. Ibid., p. 5 (italics mine).

28. For example, see David Burrell's account of analogical argument in his "Argument in Theology: Analogy and Narrative" in *New Dimensions in Philosophical Theology*, ed. Carl Raschke (Chico, Calif.: Scholars Press, 1982). Burrell argues, "The difference between ambiguous and analogous expression lies in using them systematically — that is, so as to show how the many uses can be related to one. We accomplish this, quite simply, by giving an example. Yet since examples are not ordinarily produced — as in kindergarten show-and-tell — but narrated, what we in fact do when we give an instance is tell a story."

See also Nicholas Lash, "Ideology, Metaphor, and Analogy," in *The Philosophical Frontiers of Christian Theology*, ed. B. Hebblethwaite and S. Sutherland (New York: Cambridge University Press, 1982), for an extremely nuanced account of the relation between narrative and metaphysics.

29. Gilbert Meilaender, "Against Abortion: A Protestant Proposal," *The Linacre Quarterly* 45 (May 1978), 169.

30. For some reason those concerned with the validity or invalidity of the "Divine command theory" insist on ignoring this simple fact.

31. Stanley Hauerwas, *Vision and Virtue: Essays in Christian Ethical Reflection* (reprint, Notre Dame, Ind.: University of Notre Dame Press, 1981), p. 2.

32. I am acutely aware that the issues raised here require a much fuller discussion of hermeneutics than I am able to supply. However, for a position with which I have much sympathy see Charles Wood, *The Formation of Christian Understanding: An Essay in Theological Hermeneutics* (Philadelphia: Westminster Press, 1981). Wood's discussion of the nature of canonicity seems to me to be particularly fruitful. For example, he suggests, "The form of the canon itself may indicate something of its mode of functioning. When one regards the biblical canon as a whole, the centrality to it of a narrative element is difficult to overlook: not only the chronological sweep of

the whole, from creation to new creation, including the various events and developments of what has sometimes been called 'salvation history,' but also the way the large narrative portions interweave and provide a context for the remaining materials so that they, too, have a place in the ongoing story, while these other materials—parables, hymns, prayers, summaries, theological expositions—serve in different ways to enable readers to get hold of the story and to live their way into it. This overall narrative character of the canon, together with its designation as Word of God, suggests that the canon might plausibly be construed as a story which has God as its 'author.' It is a story in which real events and persons are depicted in a way that discloses their relationship to God and to God's purposes; a story that finally involves and relates all persons and events, and which, as it is told and heard in the power of God's Spirit, becomes the vehicle of God's own definitive self-disclosure. God is not only the author of this story but its chief character as well; so that as the story unfolds we come to understand who God is. And because God is not only the chief character but also the author, the story's disclosure is God's self-disclosure. We become acquainted with God as the one who is behind this story and within it. The canon, thus construed, norms Christian witness not by providing sample statements by which to test other statements, nor by providing ideals of some other sort, but by reminding the community of the identity of the one whose word they bear" (pp. 100–101).

33. For a fuller working out of this suggestion see Patrick Sherry, "Philosophy and the Saints," *Heythrop Journal* 18 (1977), 23–37.

5. JESUS: THE PRESENCE OF THE PEACEABLE KINGDOM

1. For just one example see A. E. Harvey, *Jesus and the Constraints of History* (Philadelphia: Westminster, 1982), p. 84.

2. Jesus' emphasis on the Kingdom in itself was not unique. As Sean Freyne suggests, "According to Acts 5:33–39 such an influential Pharisaic scribe as Gamaliel I, Paul's teacher, was prepared to let the new movement take its course and attempt to authenticate its claims that it was from God. At Qumran the teacher of righteousness and his followers clearly experienced the presence of the new age in their own community which they can describe as 'the covenant which God established with Israel forever in the land of Damascus.' Throughout the whole first century a series of Zealot leaders presented themselves as messianic figures who were about to launch the final holy war against evil. . . . In itself then, there was nothing startlingly new in the proclamation of God's kingly rule, even in its final phase,

as present and operative." *The World of the New Testament* (Wilmington, Del.: Michael Glazier, 1980), p. 139.

3. See Gerza Vermes's cautions about the language of Christology for analysis of the Gospels. Gerza Vermes, "The Gospels without Christology," in *God Incarnate: Story and Belief*, ed. A. E. Harvey (London: SPCK, 1981), pp. 55–68. It may be objected that the Pauline writings stand as clear evidence against the claim made here. However I would argue that though Paul's letters do not provide the details about Jesus' life as do the Gospels, they in fact presuppose those details. Moreover Paul's scheme of redemption, his eschatology, is nothing less than the story of God that makes Jesus' life from birth to the resurrection essential for that scheme's coherence.

4. Athanasius, *The Incarnation of the Word of God* (New York: Macmillan, 1946), p. 34.

5. I am indebted to Dr. Rowan Greer for this interpretation of the Patristic understanding of the incarnation.

6. E. J. Tinsley, *The Imitation of God in Christ* (London, S.C.M. Press, 1960), p. 31.

7. Ibid., p. 35.

8. Ibid., p. 55.

9. Here, Tinsley is quoting from H. H. Rowley's *The Unity of the Bible*, p. 25.

10. Ibid., p. 61.

11. Ibid., pp. 86–87. The strong emphasis on the continuity between Jesus and Israel may be felt to be misleading exactly in terms of the central theme of this book — namely, nonviolence. For the depiction of war and violence in the Hebrew Scriptures continues to underwrite the crude, but still powerful picture held by many, that the God of the Old Testament is one of wrath and vengeance compared to the New Testament God of mercy and love. Yet those who hold this picture often, ironically, appeal to the Hebrew Scriptures to justify Christian approval of war. It is beyond the scope of this book to attempt to challenge this understanding of war in the Hebrew Scripture. However see Millard Lind, *Yahweh Is a Warrior: The Theology of Warfare in Ancient Israel* (Scottsdale, Pa.: Herald Press, 1980), for a carefully developed argument that makes views such as the above exigetically doubtful. Lind argues that "Yahweh the warrior fought by means of miracle, not through the armies of his people; 'it was not by your sword or by your bow' (Josh. 24:12). By miracle we mean an act of deliverance that was outside of Israel's control, beyond the manipulation of any human agency. This conviction was so emphatic that Israel's fighting, while at times a sequel to the act of Yahweh, was regarded ineffective; faith meant that Israel should rely upon Yahweh's miracle for her defense, rather than upon

soldiers and weapons. The human agent in the work of Yahweh was not so much the warrior as the prophet" (p. 23).

12. John Howard Yoder, *The Original Revolution* (Scottsdale, Pa.: Herald Press, 1971), pp. 1–32. Thus Yoder argues "To repent is not to feel bad but to think differently. Protestantism, and perhaps especially evangelical Protestantism, in its concern for helping every individual to make his own authentic choice in full awareness and sincerity, is in constant danger of confusing the kingdom itself with the benefits of the kingdom. If anyone repents, if anyone turns around to follow Jesus in his new way of life, this will do something for the aimlessness of his life. It will do something for his loneliness by giving him fellowship. . . . So the Bultmanns and the Grahams whose 'evangelism' is to proclaim the offer of restored selfhood, liberation from anxiety and guilt, are not wrong. . . . *But all of this is not the Gospel*. This is just the bonus, the wrapping paper thrown in when you buy the meat, the 'everything' which will be added, without our taking thought for it, if we seek first the kingdom of God and His righteousness."

13. Donald Mickie and David Rhoads, *Mark As Story* (Philadelphia: Fortress Press, 1982), p. 109.

14. Ibid., p. 111.

15. The current concern about nuclear war as a threat to end all life in some ways makes our situation similar to that of the early Christians. For example, see my "Eschatology and Nuclear Disarmament," *NICM Journal* 8, 1 (Winter 1983), pp. 7–16.

16. Harvey, *Jesus and the Constraints of History*, pp. 71–72.

17. Ibid., p. 91. Harvey argues, "New Testament scholars, who seem agreed at last that Jesus' Kingdom-sayings contain statements that are both irreducibly future and irreducibly present, tend to speak at this point of a tension between the 'already' and the 'not yet'; and indeed some tension of this kind is inevitable whenever the phrase 'the Kingdom of God' is used. For it is in reality nothing more than the abstract noun corresponding to the factual statement that God is king, which itself carries the same tension between present and future. That God is king, here and now, no believer would dream of denying. But if asked whether God is yet fully king, whether the world as we know it now is the perfect paradigm of his kingship, the believer who stands in the tradition of the Bible would be bound to say there is a sense in which God is not yet king. His kingdom is not yet universally acknowledged by his creatures. . . . The tension between the already and the not-yet is an academic tension to which nothing real corresponds, either in the experience of life or in the teaching of Jesus."

18. John Riches, *Jesus and the Transformation of Judaism* (London: Darton, Longman & Todd, 1980), pp. 93–94. See Lind for a fuller account of this understanding of the holy war tradition.

19. Riches, *Jesus and the Transformation of Judaism*, p. 95.

20. Harvey, *Jesus and the Constraints of History*, p. 86.

21. Ibid., p. 51.

22. The question of Jesus' continuity and discontinuity with the various forms of Judaism of his day is not easily resolved. Certainly most of Jesus' message was in continuity with what Israel had already discovered about her relation with God. The decisive difference was that now that relation turned on the life of this man Jesus, and that put him in quite different ways in conflict with the various groups of his day. As Sean Fryne notes, "By claiming that the divine presence, defined both as God's kingly rule and as Father, was accessible to people in his own life and person, Jesus undercut the various systems that had been devised within Judaism to control that presence and people's access to it. Therein lay the source of power within actual Palestinian life for parties like the Pharisees and Sadducees, and the aspirations to power of other groups like the Essenes and Zealots. Insofar as Jesus' claims suggested alternative means of access to God, or better, of God's coming to people, outside and independently of all of the groups and their programmes, and to the extent that this had been found attractive, he was clearly striking at the very reasons for existence of each of the groups and their philosophies. To do so in the name of God's final and irrevocable promises to his people was intolerable." *The World of the New Testament*, p. 140.

23. Riches, *Jesus and the Transformation of Judaism*, p. 106.

24. John Yoder, *The Original Revolution*, p. 42.

25. For an often overlooked but classic account of the relation between forgiveness and our ability to recount our history, see H. R. Niebuhr, *The Meaning of Revelation* (New York: Macmillan, 1960), pp. 82–90.

26. Rowan Williams, *Resurrection* (London: Darton, Longman & Todd, 1982), p. 49.

27. Ibid., p. 85.

6. THE SERVANT COMMUNITY: CHRISTIAN SOCIAL ETHICS

1. The classic statement of this view remains G. H. Mead's, *Mind, Self, and Society* (Chicago: University of Chicago Press, 1934). For a recent attempt to restate this insight while preserving a sense of agency, see Howard Harrod, *The Human Center: Moral Agency in the Social World* (Philadelphia: Fortress Press, 1981).

2. There is a crucial relation, not often noticed, between this understanding of authority and the question of the unity of the virtues. For I do not believe that the virtues form a unity, either for individuals or com-

munities, since there is no single principle from which they can be derived or ordered. Therefore differences and potential conflict cannot be excluded from good communities. Indeed the very diversity of the virtues, and corresponding lives, is required if the church is to have the resources necessary for being faithful to the many-sided tale that constitutes "Scripture."

3. John Howard Yoder, *The Original Revolution* (Scottsdale, Pa.: Herald Press, 1971), p. 116.

The reality designated "world" is obviously an extremely complex phenomenon. In the New Testament it is often used to designate that order organized and operating devoid of any reference to God's will. This is particularly true of the Johannine corpus. Yet the world is nonetheless described as the object of God's love (John 3:16) and even in 1 John, Jesus is called the "savior of the world" (4:14). The world, therefore, even in the Johannine literature is not depicted as completely devoid of God's presence and/or good order. The great problem, as well as temptation, is to assume that we have a clear idea what empirical subject, i.e., government, society, etc., that corresponds to the Johannine description. That is why I think Yoder so wisely locates the basis for the distinction between church and world in agents rather than ontological orders or institutions. To do so makes clear that: (1) the distinction between church and world runs through every agent and thus there is no basis for self-righteousness on the part of those who explicitly identify with the church; and (2) that the "necessities" many claim must be accepted as part and parcel of being "world," such as violence, are such only because of our unfaithfulness. Thus the world, when it is true to its nature as God's redeemed subject, can be ordered and governed without resort to violence.

4. I am obviously drawing here on the work of H. R. Niebuhr. See in particular his *The Responsible Self* (New York: Harper & Row, 1963).

5. James Gustafson's *Treasures in Earthen Vessels* (New York: Harper & Row, 1961) still provides the best analysis of the church as a "natural" institution. Moreover, particularly important for the development of this insight in a normative direction is Gustafson's too often overlooked *The Church as Moral Decision-Maker* (Philadelphia: Pilgrim Press, 1976). The general position I am trying to defend is nicely summarized by Karl Barth. He says "the decisive contribution which the Christian community can make to the upbuilding and work and maintenance of the civil consists in the witness which it has to give to it and to all human societies in the form of the order of its own upbuilding and constitution. It cannot give in the world a direct portrayal of Jesus Christ, who is also the world's Lord and Savior, or of the peace and freedom and joy of the kingdom of God. For it is itself only a human society moving like all others to His

manifestation. But in the form in which it exists among them it can and must be to the world of men around it a reminder of the law of the kingdom of God already set up on earth in Jesus Christ, and a promise of its future manifestation. *De facto*, whether they realise it or not, it can and should show them that there is already on earth an order which is based on the great alteration of the human situation and directed towards its manifestation." Karl Barth, *Church Dogmatics*, IV/2, trans. G. W. Bromiley (Edinburgh: T. & T. Clark, 1958), p. 721. A few pages later Barth suggests that "If the community were to imagine that the reach of the sanctification of humanity accomplished in Jesus Christ were restricted to itself and the ingathering of believers, that it did not have corresponding effects *extra muros ecclesiae*, it would be in flat contradiction to its own confession of its Lord" (p. 723).

That the church is a natural institution in no way lessens the demands the church puts on any society in which it finds itself—not the least of which is the demand for the free preaching of the gospel. No society, or state, is so far from God's care that it cannot in principle recognize the legitimacy of this claim. Of course the form of their "freedom" can vary and certainly those societies that have translated the necessity of the church's freedom into special legal status for the church, or religion, suggest that such status usually results in a self-willed loss of freedom by the church. The demand of the church to be free is always more a demand placed on the church to be a people distinctive enough to make their "freedom" interesting than a demand placed on society.

6. James Gustafson, *Christian Ethics and the Community* (Philadelphia: Pilgrim Press, 1971), pp. 153–163. That all human relations require and engender some sense of trust indicates why the virtues require narrative construal. For without the latter the very skills necessary for us to be good can be made to serve our most destructive capacities. Sensing that, too often we try to avoid trusting anyone or anything and as a result become subject to the most oppressive tyrant—ourselves.

7. Thus John Howard Yoder argues, "any renunciation of violence is preferable to its acceptance; but what Jesus renounced is not first of all violence, but rather the compulsiveness of purpose that leads men to violate the dignity of others. The point is not that one can attain all of one's legitimate ends without using violent means. It is rather that our readiness to renounce our legitimate ends whenever they cannot be attained by legitimate means itself constitutes our participation in the triumphant suffering of the Lamb." *The Politics of Jesus* (Grand Rapids, Mich.: Eerdmans, 1972), pp. 243–244.

8. John Howard Yoder, *The Original Revolution*, p. 121. It is instructive to compare this with Michael Novak's critique of the Catholic bishops

on nuclear disarmament. Novak explicitly asserts the "Christian faith does not teach us to rely on the miraculous." "Making Deterrence Work," *Catholicism in Crisis* 1/1 (November 1982), p. 5.

9. This way of putting the matter I have borrowed from Paul Van Buren's *Discerning the Way* (New York: Seabury Press, 1980).

10. As William Willimon says, "The Lord's Supper is a 'sanctifying ordinance,' a sign of the continuity, necessity, and availability of God's enabling, communal, confirming, nurturing grace. Our characters are formed, sanctified, by such instruments of continual divine activity in our lives. Sanctification is a willingness to see our lives as significant only as we are formed into God's image for us. According to Paul, that image is always ecclesial, social, communal. In our attentiveness and response to this call to be saints, we find our thoughts, affections, sight, and deeds qualified by this beckoning grace. We become characterized as those who attend to the world in a different way from those who are not so qualified. Gradually we are weaned from our natural self-centered, autonomous ways of looking at the world until we become as we profess. We are different." *The Service of God: How Worship and Ethics are Related* (Nashville: Abingdon Press, 1983), p. 125.

11. Enda McDonagh, *Doing the Truth: The Quest for Moral Theology* (Notre Dame, Ind.: University of Notre Dame Press, 1979), pp. 40–57.

12. Vincent Donovan, *Christianity Rediscovered* (Maryknoll, N.Y.: Orbis Books, 1982), p. 125. I am indebted to Philip Foubert for calling Donovan's fascinating book to my attention.

13. Donovan, p. 127.

14. Enda McDonagh, *Church and Politics* (Notre Dame, Ind.: University of Notre Dame Press, 1980), p. 27.

15. Yoder, *The Original Revolution*, pp. 165–166. For Yoder's fuller analysis of the theological status of democracy see his "The Christian Case for Democracy," *Journal of Religious Ethics* 5 (Fall 1977), 209–224.

16. McDonagh, *Church and Politics*, p. 34.

17. McDonagh is quite right to stress the importance of the distinction between state and society, for there is no doubt it has proved crucial for securing more nearly just social orders. Moreover, there is every reason to think this distinction between state and society—i.e., the assumption that society is a moral reality more primary than the organ of government, thus making the latter subordinate to, as well as a service for, the former—is the result of the Christian challenge to the authority of the Roman imperium. Yet it cannot, therefore, be concluded that the Church has more stake in social orders that seem to maintain in theory a "limited" state than in those that do not. For no state is more omnivorous in its appetites for our loyalty

than one that claims it is protecting our freedom from "state-control." See McDonagh, ibid., pp. 29–39.

18. Ibid., p. 69.

19. To what extent Christians can or can not participate in a society's government cannot be determined in principle but depends on the character and nature of individual societies and their governments. Most governmental functions, even within the military, do not depend on coercion and violence. It may be possible, therefore, for a Christian in some societies to be a policeman, prison warden, etc. What, however, is crucial is that Christians work to help their societies develop the kind of people and institutions that make possible a government that can be just without resort to violence.

7. CASUISTRY AS A NARRATIVE ART

1. Mary Douglass, *Purity and Danger: An Analysis of Concepts of Pollution and Taboo* (London: Routledge and Kegan Paul, 1966), p. 39. Paul Ramsey also calls attention to the Nuer in his "Abortion: A Review Article," *The Thomist* 37/1 (January 1973), p. 203.

2. Indeed, from this perspective the issue is what kind of quandaries we ought to have as a people. The virtuous are not free from quandaries, but the *kind* of quandaries they confront result from the kind of people they are.

3. Alasdair MacIntyre, "Theology, Ethics, and the Ethics of Medicine and Health Care," *Journal of Medicine and Philosophy* 4/4 (December 1979), p. 437.

4. Thus Aristotle suggests that we become just by acting the way just people act. *Nichomachean Ethics*, trans. Martin Ostwald (Indianapolis: Bobbs-Merrill, 1962), 1105a25–1105b10.

5. Though I am not sure where she said it, I am sure this quote is from Iris Murdock. See in particular her *The Sovereignty of Good* (New York: Schocken Books, 1970).

6. John Howard Yoder, "What Would You Do If?" *Journal of Religious Ethics* 2/1 (Fall 1974), pp. 82–83.

7. Ibid., p. 86.

8. Ibid., p. 87.

9. Ibid., p. 90.

10. Ibid., p. 94.

11. Ibid., pp. 96–97.

12. Ibid., p. 99.

13. Ibid., pp. 100–101.

14. Ibid., p. 101.

15. For a defense of this interpretation of More's life see Thomas Shaffer's and my article, "Hope Faces Power: Thomas More and the King of England," *Soundings* 61 (Winter 1978), 456–479.

16. It may be objected that the issue really is not one of lying at all, but rather adultery. For my friend could have had a brief encounter with the stewardess and then come home and told his wife the truth. He might have done that and his wife might even have been willing to accept his infidelity. But the point is she should not accept such a "truth" for both he and she would then be expecting less of their marriage than they should. In that sense the issue is adultery insofar as adultery is a reminder of the kind of faithfulness demanded of Christians in marriage as a condition of marriage being a truthful institution. So my example does depend on a normative view of marriage that I have not here defended. It is, however, one I would defend since I believe that questions of faithfulness in marriage and truthfulness are closely connected.

17. Yoder, p. 101.

18. James Gustafson has developed the significance of moral discourse more fully than anyone. See his *The Church as a Moral Decision-Maker* (Philadelphia: Pilgrim Press, 1970). In his *Decision Making in the Church: A Biblical Model* (Philadelphia: Fortress Press, 1983), Luke Johnson, by an analysis of Acts, shows how the early church arrived at its decisions through a narrative process. Thus the decision made at the Jerusalem conference in Acts 15 is only intelligible in the light of Cornelius' conversion.

19. Aristotle, *Nichomachean Ethics*, 1098a5–1098b7.

20. For example, Charles Wood reminds us that "understanding a text" is no single thing nor is it captured by any one method. Rather understanding masks a variety of abilities which may be demonstrated in various ways. Thus the task of understanding Christianity may turn out to be more arduous than we had anticipated. The reason for this, according to Wood, is "that some of the concepts central to Christian teaching are rather complex, existentially rooted concepts whose acquisition entails particular kinds of moral and emotional growth. Such concepts as gratitude or joy have conceptual prerequisites, in that, for example, a capacity for gratitude presupposes a particular awareness of self and other, and a capacity for joy presupposes the capacity to care. So to learn these characteristically Christian concepts and thus to 'understand Christianity,' involves one in what may be a fairly intensive and thoroughgoing education in human existence, particularly if one's education has been somewhat spotty up to this point." *The Formation of Christian Understanding: An Essay in Theological Hermeneutics* (Philadelphia: Westminster Press, 1981), pp. 24–25.

21. A "lively memory" is one that continues to test our moral notions

by analogical comparison. For casuistry is but an extended discussion of the significance of certain notions by testing them continually against new sets of circumstances and/or in relation to other notions. For example, the development of respiration therapy rightly required us to rethink what we meant by euthanasia—or better, it helped us better understand what we felt was morally at stake in prohibiting euthanasia. How euthanasia is similar to or different from suicide must then be considered; and whether suicide and euthanasia are both but species of murder must be discussed. Finally, we cannot avoid theological discussion of how these forms of life-taking relate to our conviction that God, and not ourselves, is the final Lord of our lives. It is exactly that question that may determine why certain forms of letting die should *not* be called euthanasia.

I am indebted to Mr. David Schmidt for reminding me of the importance of analogy for casuistry.

8. TRAGEDY AND JOY: THE SPIRITUALITY OF PEACEABLENESS

1. H. Richard Niebuhr, "The Grace of Doing Nothing," *Christian Century* 49 (March 23, 1932), 378–380.

2. Reinhold Niebuhr, "Must We Do Nothing?" *Christian Century* 49 (March 30, 1932), 415–417.

3. H. Richard Niebuhr, p. 378.

4. Ibid., p. 379.

5. Ibid.

6. Ibid.

7. Ibid., p. 380.

8. Reinhold Niebuhr, p. 416.

9. Ibid.

10. Ibid.

11. Ibid., p. 417.

12. Ibid. It is interesting that Reinhold Niebuhr insists on characterizing H. Richard Niebuhr's position in his own language—i.e., "pure love." H. Richard Niebuhr did not use that language in his article or his books, but he developed the eschatological emphasis. The deeper difference between the two brothers is thus not over nonviolence as the norm of the Christian life, but involves the basic theological terms that set the context for the Christian's understanding of the world. Thus, in a letter responding to his brother's article, H. Richard Niebuhr suggests the issue is not really a choice between activity or inactivity, since they are really speaking of two kinds of activity. "The fundamental question seems to me to be whether 'the

history of mankind is a perennial tragedy' which can derive meaning only from a goal which lies beyond history, as my brother maintains, or whether the 'eschatological' faith, to which I seek to adhere, is justifiable. In that faith tragedy is only the prelude to fulfilment and a prelude which is necessary because of human nature; the kingdom of God comes inevitably, though whether we shall see it or not depends on our recognition of its presence and our acceptance of the only kind of life which will enable us to enter it, the life of repentence and forgiveness." "A Communication: The Only Way into the Kingdom of God," *Christian Century* 49 (April 6, 1932), 447.

13. For an insightful treatment of Reinhold Niebuhr as providing the theological justification for a spirituality sufficient to sustain a realistic Christian social ethic see Dennis McCann, *Christian Realism and Liberation Theology* (Maryknoll, N.Y.: Orbis Books, 1981).

14. Reinhold Niebuhr, p. 417.

15. For further reflections on this issue see my "On Surviving Justly: An Ethical Analysis of Nuclear Disarmament," *Religious Conscience and Nuclear Warfare*, ed. Jill Raitt (Columbia, Missouri: University of Missouri Press, forthcoming).

16. For an extraordinary account of how violence is at the basis of our social life see René Girard, *Des choses cachées depuis la fondation du monde* (Paris: Grasset, 1978).

17. I am indebted to Edward Santouri for helping me see the difference between a sense of tragedy and the claim that the moral life inherently involves tragic dilemmas. The former does not necessarily entail the strong latter claim, though I remain unconvinced that some account of tragic choices is not required for an adequate account of our moral existence.

For an extremely interesting account of how tragedy can qualify an account of the virtues see John Barbour, "Tragedy and Ethical Reflection," *Journal of Religion* 63/1 (January 1983), pp. 1–28. Barbour makes the important point that because of its very nature we cannot "choose" to have a "tragic sense of life," for tragedy is only real when it is not chosen but is unavoidable. Therefore I am not recommending that Christians have or ought to have a "tragic sense," but rather that we are committed to the kind of life that makes tragic outcomes unavoidable. That is why we require patience to face the tragic but the hope that it can be avoided.

18. Reinhold Niebuhr, *Beyond Tragedy* (New York: Charles Scribner's Sons, 1937), p. 169.

19. There is still no better account of happiness than Aristotle's often misunderstood treatment. For happiness is finally not so much something we desire, in Aristotle's rendering of it, as it is that which comes at the end of a life well lived—that is, a life that has been formed rightly by the right

Index